JULIE LEFEBURE

RIGHT NOW MATTERS

Empowering Right-Now Women in a Culture of Distraction

Cover & interior design by Typewriter Creative Co.
Cover photo by @AngrySun

ISBN 979-8-9890693-0-9 (Paperback)
ISBN 979-8-9890693-1-6 (eBook)

In a world constantly vying for our attention, *Right Now Matters* is a beacon of hope for anyone seeking to overcome distraction and live a God-glorifying life. Julie offers relatable examples from her own life, research-backed strategies, and sound Biblical teaching to help you regain your focus. With journaling prompts, she also helps you pause and reflect on the areas where you need the most help in overcoming distraction. This book is not just a guide; it's a game-changer as you become a Right-Now Woman!

—JENNIFER DUKES LEE,
author of *Growing Slow* and *Stuff I'd Only Tell God*

If you've ever missed a key moment in a loved one's life because you were too distracted to notice, this book is for you! I highly recommend *Right Now Matters* by Julie Lefebure because it offers easy, practical tools for overcoming distractions so we can live in the presence of God today. *Right Now Matters* graciously guides the reader to be intentionally present in the right now and make an eternal impact by avoiding the lure of distraction. This book will help increase the quality and effectiveness of your life as you embrace living undistracted!

—NICOLE WILLIAMS,
author of *Rise Up: Believing God When the World is Falling Apart*

Julie Lefebure does a great job of showing us how to recognize the distractions in our lives that keep us from having the ability to draw closer to God. By conquering those things that distract us, we're able to think about the present and live the life the Lord has planned for us. To help us understand the harm of distractions, she shares Bible verses, examples of her personal experiences, and the tools she has used to stay focused on what's happening "right now." The Scripture, her experiences, and her many tools are easy to understand, simple to use, and effective.

—REVEREND BARBARA ROSE FURMAN,
author of *It Is Well With My Soul: My Story*

For a world plagued by an epidemic of distraction, Julie Lefebure shares her personal struggles and triumphs, along with practical solutions, and most importantly the path to freedom through Hope in Christ. In all the ways, and for all the reasons so sentimentally shared in this book — Right. Now. Matters.

—MEREDITH BERNARD

This Farm Wife

Are you living distracted? I know this is a struggle for me, so I am thankful for Julie Lefebure's book, *Right Now Matters*. As I read through the pages, I can relate to her stories, specifically missing a son's goal while being physically present but not emotionally. Her honesty and transparency coupled with the practical tools and tips in her book will help all of us to live in the moment and be intentional with our loved ones. This book is a must read if you, too, need help living undistracted in the Right Now moment.

—JODI ROSSER,

author of *Depth: Growing Through Heartbreak to Strength*

To Bill, Alissa, Morgan, Nolan,
Griffin, Zach, and Paige.
Because of your constant presence,
love, support, and encouragement,
you help me be a Right-Now Woman.
You inspire me daily, and
I love you more than you know.

Contents

Introduction...9
    Distracted and Devastated: My Journey to
    Discovering the Gift of Every Moment

1 The Importance of Right Now..........................15
    What if we embrace life right now,
    even if we do it imperfectly?

2 There's Got to Be More 29
    What if we focus on living our lives abundantly?

3 Too Busy to Notice 41
    What if we remove the word busy from our lives?

4 Distractions Everywhere...............................53
    What if we address our distractions to overcome them?

5 The Big Five 67
    What if we understand living distracted
    is not what's best for us?

6 A Different Way..83
    What if we could overcome distractions
    by partnering with God?

7   Embrace Each Day 95
What if we begin our day with God?

8   Enjoy Peaceful Rest 107
What if we end our day with God?

9   Tools to Refocus 119
What if we could overcome distractions
by using simple tools?

10 Things Above 131
What if we keep our focus on what's most important?

11 Helpful Diversions 143
What if distractions could help us?

12 Not Always About Us 155
What if we desire to bless others by living undistracted?

13 Our Trowel and Sword 165
What if we pray as we work?

14 Right-Now Women 177
What if we live as Right-Now Women?

Appendix 193

Notes 195

Acknowledgments 199

About the Author 203

Introduction

Distracted and Devastated:

My Journey to Discovering the Gift of Every Moment

I remember the moment vividly. Sitting in the stands, it thrilled me to watch my son play soccer, his favorite high school sport. I'm the mom who always tries to show up for every one of my kids' activities—even in their adulthood. It's important to me, and I believe it's important to them. My son, in his number eleven white-and-orange jersey, was my focus on the field that day—until he wasn't. My mind started wandering to my growing to-do list, the next thing on my schedule, and what I'd be doing later that evening. While my thoughts were pinballing from one thing to the next, my ears caught the roar of the crowd. Jolted back to the game, I realized I missed a moment I would never be able to relive: I missed my son's amazing play.

Immense regret consumed me as everyone cheered and offered congratulatory glances toward me and my husband. I pretended I didn't miss my son's goal and cheered right along with every other fan. But inside, my heart sank. It felt heavier than a two-ton truck, and I wished to turn back time for a do-over. I couldn't believe it. *No, no, no! How did I miss this one moment? Seriously, I am sitting right here in the stands with everyone else. I'm here to watch Zach, but I missed his incredible play.* I was present, yet I wasn't. My thoughts took me away for a few short seconds, just long enough to distract me from the moment. An extremely important moment, and one I will never get back.

It became clear to me right then: I had a problem. I was living distracted. Oh, I had known this for quite some time, I just hadn't named it as such. This wasn't the first time I had experienced this kind of occurrence. It was one of several. Frankly, I was weary of how easily my attention switched to something other than the present moment.

I know I'm not the only one. A multitude of us are missing the special moments happening right in front of us: the blooming flower poking through the crack in the sidewalk, the amber-and-coral-streaked sunrise, the encouraging words from a friend, the innocent laughter from our children, or the loving glance from our spouse.

Distracted living occurs anytime something causes us to shift our focus from the present. Surprisingly, it can be just as dangerous as distracted driving. Regardless of what steals our attention, our awareness of the present moment diminishes, and it's not just when we're behind the wheel.

Distractions interrupt our lives and pull us away from living in the present, from staying in the *right now*. And the thing is, right now is what each of us has in our possession. Right now is the most important moment, because it's the one we're currently living. Not yesterday and not tomorrow. All we have is right now. Right now matters.

When you think about the distractions that entice you away from right now, what are they? When you're having a conversation with someone, what distracts you and makes your mind wander? When you're immersed in a project at work, what distraction interrupts your workflow? When you're playing with your children, what deters you from the beautiful moment you are in? When you find a few moments for yourself to sit quietly, what invades your thoughts and coaxes you to get moving again?

Is it your phone or device? Are notifications buzzing or dinging, making you think you're missing something important? Is your schedule jam-packed and overwhelming your thoughts? Do reminders of your past distract you in the present? Or do worries about the future pull you away from today? Do your dreams and goals divert you from living right now?

You are not alone. In fact, most of us are right there with you. But you and I aren't left without hope. We can do something about this problem. We can make different choices than the ones we're currently making. We can intentionally choose to live differently, to live undistracted. It begins with right now.

After missing my son's play that day, I mentally drew a line in the sand. Still filled with regret as I sat there the remainder of the game, I declared I would not allow such a thing to happen again. I would not miss another special moment as a result of living distracted.

That was the spring of 2015. I can fully disclose I am a work in progress, and I have not yet mastered the art of living undistracted. Since that day, I have missed additional special moments because of distractions. But I have learned from these moments, and because of them, I have taught myself ways to stay present. I am now more aware of what lures me away the easiest, and I'm more mindful of how quickly my thoughts can be snatched elsewhere. I've also learned how to recognize when distractions entice me from living in the present and consciously choose to remain engaged.

Learning a new way of living takes time. It doesn't happen overnight, even if we wish it, will it, or want it to happen quickly. Learning to live undistracted is a daily battle, and it will likely remain that way for me this side of eternity. It takes dedicated effort and intention. But living undistracted in the present is a beautiful gift worth the effort.

I invite you to join me in this endeavor to journey with me in the quest to live undistracted, to learn the value of right now, and to stay present in it. This shift to take back our lives and thrive in the present can start now. You and I can stop distractions from taking over our minds and, essentially, our lives. Our lives and the moments we are given are too valuable to miss.

In the pages ahead, we will find the help, hope, and encouragement we need to take the steps necessary to live undistracted. We will uncover and address several of the distractions we encounter daily. In doing so, we will learn the ultimate source of these distractions—and the secret to combating them. We will access helpful tools and tricks I've taught myself over the last several years in the pursuit to live undistracted. And we will discover what God says about distractions and the hope He offers us in spite of them.

We will also learn what it means to be Right-Now Women, we who focus on the right-now moment. Not just for ourselves but to make a difference in this world and to impact the lives of those around us.

At the end of each chapter you'll find space to incorporate a tool I use on a daily basis. It's called the Four Ps: Pause, Ponder, Pray, and Praise. We discuss this in greater detail in Chapter 9, but this tool is a perfect way to apply what we're learning in each chapter as we go. (Feel free to jump to Chapter 9 for greater detail.)

The Pause section invites you to pause briefly to bring your focus back to that chapter's subject with a prompt or suggestion. The Ponder section offers a reflection. The Pray section encourages you to have a conversation with God with prompts. The Praise section reminds you to lift your focus to praise and thank God.

Right now matters, and how we live in this moment matters. Together we will learn how to embrace each moment and live the abundant life God wants us to live. Ready? Let's take the next step together.

1

THE IMPORTANCE
OF RIGHT NOW

*What if we embrace life right now,
even if we do it imperfectly?*

M y husband, Bill, loves to bicycle. He has for as long as I've
known him, and that's a long time. During the last full week
of July here in Iowa, cyclists from all over the world descend on our
state for the week-long bicycle ride across Iowa called RAGBRAI
(Register's Annual Great Bicycle Ride Across Iowa). Before we married, Bill rode his mint-green bicycle, fondly named "The Beast," for
numerous years on the ride. The year we met—also the year before
we married—I bought a turquoise Schwinn bicycle for $350 three
days before RAGBRAI. I surprised Bill by riding one day of the ride
with him. Let me tell you, two days of training isn't enough for a six-
ty-mile ride in one day. At least it wasn't for me and my backside. I
couldn't sit down for days!

After we married, however, bicycling for Bill took a backseat to
family and farming. It wasn't until twenty-one years later in the
summer of 2013, Bill decided to dust off The Beast and ride it on

RAGBRAI once again. From the comforts of our home, I cheered him on as he made his way across Iowa that July.

He continued riding after completing RAGBRAI, training to do a local 100-mile ride a few weeks later. On a quiet Saturday morning, he was pedaling on a paved rural two-lane road. In the distance through his rearview mirror, he noticed a white car approaching, so he and The Beast hugged the road's outside white line. The next thing he knew, he was catapulting into the air. The car's passenger side mirror caught Bill's left backside, sending him airborne. The Beast's front wheel popped the car's right front tire. Bill landed thirty feet away, face down on the road's shoulder.

The impact knocked the wind out of him. Lying there, trying desperately to fill his lungs with air, his thoughts turned to me and our kids, uncertain if he would ever see us again.

When one encounters a near-death experience or an experience like my husband's, perspective on life shifts, and what truly matters comes into full view. Maybe you've had a similar experience or know someone who has. What was important to Bill—his family—is what he thought of while lying on the gravel pebbles lining the road.

What would fill our minds if you or I were the ones lying there, trying to catch our breath? Would we think of the daily, mundane things that consume our minds, or would our thoughts be of the people and the important relationships in our lives? What *is* important to us in this life? This is a good question to ask ourselves because our answers reflect our priorities. And maybe where we place our focus—the daily frustrations, distractions, confounding circumstances—isn't so important after all. Maybe our material possessions, our fame and fortune, or our achievements aren't what really matters in the big scheme of things.

So what is important in life? I invite you to pause here and answer this for yourself. This question helps us to understand the gift of each moment and decide how we fill our time. I get how easy it is to take these moments for granted. We can forget how priceless they truly are, can't we? Yet, when we pause and ponder this question, we comprehend how our lives are made up of umpteen incredible moments. This matters. Our lives matter. Right now matters.

Plenty are important in my life: my family, my health, my peace and joy. But my faith in God through Jesus Christ is my lifeline. This is what's most important to me. It's what holds me together and keeps me sane. It's my guiding light and my source of strength, hope, and truth. I imperfectly follow Jesus, and I'm grateful for His patience with me. You'll find I weave my faith throughout the tapestry of this book.

So pause, ponder, and write what is important in your life in this space. It'll help set you on the path to appreciating right now.

_____

_____

_____

_____

_____

_____

_____

_____

_____

In the book of Genesis we learn how God created day and night.[1] We understand He also created this day and this very moment. Not only that, but He's *in* this moment. Henri Nouwen wrote:

> *"The real enemies of our life are the 'oughts' and the 'ifs.' They pull us backward into the unalterable past and forward into the unpredictable future. But real life takes place in the here and the now. God is a God of the present. God is always in the moment, be that moment hard or easy, joyful or painful. When Jesus spoke about God, he always spoke about God as being where and when you are. 'When you see me, you see God. When you hear me, you hear God.' God is not someone who was or will be, but the One who is, and who is for me in the present moment. That's why Jesus came to wipe away the burden of the past and the worries of the future. He wants us to discover God right where we are, here and now."[2]*

Right now matters because it's where God is and where He desires to meet us. It's where God desires us to live, not in the past nor in the future. Right now matters because it's the only moment God is present with us.

Do you know the word "now" occurs 1,219 times in the New International Version translation of the Bible? This word, which means "at the present time or without delay," was clearly as important in Bible times as it is today.

Here are a few examples from Scripture (emphasis added):

> "And **now** these three remain: faith, hope and love. But the greatest of these is love" (1 Corinthians 13:13).

"**Now** the Lord is the Spirit, and where the Spirit of the Lord is, there is freedom" (2 Corinthians 3:17).

"For he says, 'In the time of my favor I heard you, and in the day of salvation I helped you.' I tell you, **now** is the time of God's favor, **now** is the day of salvation" (2 Corinthians 6:2).

"For you were once darkness, but **now** you are light in the Lord. Live as children of light" (Ephesians 5:8).

"**Now** may the Lord of peace himself give you peace at all times and in every way. The Lord be with all of you" (2 Thessalonians 3:16).

Right now matters.

All we have is right now and we don't get another opportunity to live this moment over.

The driver of the white car stopped with his punctured tire. A neighboring farmer heard the crash and called 911, and Bill was taken to a local hospital by ambulance. You can imagine my horror when I received Bill's call telling me he was in the hospital. Arriving there in a rush, I was thankful to find him sitting up in bed with a smile on his face. No tubes, no casts, no monitors hooked up—what a relief!

Still shaking as I drove us home from the hospital an hour later, I listened intently as Bill shared the entire ordeal. I was convinced God spared Bill's life that morning. If Bill would have flown to the left instead of the right after getting hit, he likely would have ended on or under the car. He might not have survived. I have a difficult time letting my mind play out that scenario still today. Amazingly, Bill said his head never hit the ground. His helmet didn't sustain even one single scratch! *Thank You, God.*

Sometimes it takes a shaking up to wake us up. And Bill's accident was a big wake-up call for me, and maybe for him too. His accident reminded us tomorrow isn't guaranteed. Our next moment isn't promised. All we have is right now and we don't get another opportunity to live this moment over. We don't get a do-over. We get one chance to make right now count.

When we think of life more in this way, we appreciate the treasure it is. We understand how right now matters, and we begin to embrace each moment we're given. We're less likely to take our moments for granted. We realize how we live right now really does matter.

The jolting thought of a life without my husband woke me up to reality. I was living my life and going through the motions on autopilot. I guess you could say I was sleepwalking through life, living for the weekends and numbing out with busyness the rest of the week. I wasn't living fully awake and alert, nor was I living the abundant life Jesus came to give me.

"The thief approaches *with malicious intent*, looking to steal, slaughter, and destroy; I came to give life with joy and abundance" (John 10:10 Voice).

How about you? Are you living this abundant life Jesus came to give you? Maybe you can relate to sleepwalking through life. Maybe you're realizing how life has become monotonous or even boring. Or quite possibly you've lost your joy and peace, your excitement for life. I understand. Many of us don't wake up to this reality. But when we do, we realize God has more for us than the life we're living. He's got more for us than what distractions have to offer.

We can treat every moment as a gift, opening it with excitement like a child on Christmas morning, or we can take it for granted and never get around to tearing into it. I don't know about you, but the suspense of an unwrapped gift nearly excites me to the point of annoyance. Especially if that gift is for me. Especially if it's under a Christmas tree for days and weeks in advance. *Why don't I look at each moment of the day in this same manner?*

When we choose to treat right now as the gift it is, you and I can look at what we're given through eyes of gratefulness and appreciation. We are inspired to view our daily lives as priceless gifts. When this happens, we are better able to live each moment of each day in God's abundance. And when we do that, we are less likely to live it distracted.

Have you ever tried to define a moment? Some "experts" say a moment is ninety seconds in length. A moment (momentum) was a medieval unit of time, and the earliest reference of the moment dates back to writings of an English monk in the 8th Century.[3] Yet Nobel Prize-winning scientist, Daniel Kahneman, says we experience approximately 20,000 individual moments in a waking day.[4] I'm guessing many of us consider a moment more as a brief point in time. So, for the sake of ease, let's consider a moment as a second in an hour. In a 24-hour period, we have 1,440 minutes and 86,400 seconds. So using our consideration of a moment representing a second, we each experience 86,400 moments in a day (depending how you consider a moment).

Just for fun, let's equate these 86,400 seconds (moments) into dollars. Let's say we each have 86,400 dollar bills in our bank accounts, and we can spend them on anything we want. That's pretty exciting, isn't it? How will you use this money? What will you purchase?

Some say our time is more priceless than money. As I get older, I agree more with this statement. If our time is more priceless than our money, and we have 86,400 seconds (moments) to spend and experience in a day, what will we do with them? Will we invest those seconds (moments) in what's important to us, or will we squander them away? Will we allow the distractions of this life to snatch them from us, or will we live with intention and purpose?

Miraculously, Bill's accident that Saturday morning only resulted in a few cracked ribs, some internal muscle injuries, and road rash over parts of his body. For days afterward, he was in excruciating pain. His wrists, back, and ankles still feel the effects of the accident some days. But he is here. He is alive.

Right now matters.

Even though Bill healed and is doing well today, sadly, The Beast was totaled. It didn't stand a chance against that white car at fifty-five miles per hour. Bill has countless wonderful memories on that bike, and thankfully, he was able to salvage a few parts from it. And who knows, maybe God used that old bicycle made from heavy and hearty parts to aid Bill in saving his life.

Bill's desire to bike never left him, although fear of getting back on the bike often overwhelmed him. The following winter he asked me if I would consider biking RAGBRAI with him on our tandem bicycle that next July. Remember, bicycling was his thing, not mine. We had an old 1985 tandem bicycle hanging in our garage we rode just for fun. But riding it for a week? I wasn't so sure about that.

Because I recalled how sore my backside was after only one day of biking RAGBRAI years earlier, I couldn't imagine how it would feel after seven days in a row! I thought about the Iowa July heat and humidity and sleeping in a tent for seven nights. And what about showering and eating and getting ready each morning? *What would that look like?* What about my clothes, my makeup, my morning coffee, and the other comforts of home? I desperately wanted to say no. Everything in me screamed, *no!* But it came down to this: if Bill wanted to face his fear of getting back on a bike, I wanted to do all I could to support him. *How could I say no?*

So I didn't. With uncertainty and fear, mixed with love and support, I shyly said yes. And I soon learned what my yes meant. It meant not only sleeping in a tent and standing in line for a shower for seven days, it was also rising at 5 a.m. to pedal 40-100 miles on each day's route. It meant leaving all the comforts of home behind, wearing no makeup and not doing my hair for seven days. It meant training beforehand by bicycling 1,000 miles between April and July, and it meant we would be together for seven straight days—except for bathroom breaks and showering. *Could our marriage survive that?*

We embarked on the greatest adventure together. We just didn't know how great it would be, especially me. For someone who always said bicycling wasn't my thing, I became absolutely hooked on RAGBRAI. *Who would have known?* But on this ride I saw a side of Bill I had never seen before in our twenty-one years of marriage. Don't get me wrong, he's a wise, funny, caring, loving, and laid-back kind of guy. But during RAGBRAI week, he transforms into what I describe as "a little kid on Christmas morning." He's excited, relaxed, joyful, and he laughs a whole lot more on RAGBRAI. I see a light in his eyes that isn't quite as vibrant during the rest of the year, and that light proves how important bicycling is to him. *What if I would have said no to his invitation?*

It's time we embrace each moment we're given to live in God's grace and abundance.

So, now bicycling is *our* thing. We've completed eight years of RAGBRAI on our tandem bike as of this writing. While on the ride, I also appreciate that we completely live in the moment with no distractions. We aren't on a schedule. We eat when we're hungry, and we go to bed when we're tired. We get to be ourselves with no commitments or deadlines. And I don't have to fuss with makeup or do my hair. (I already shared that, didn't I? That's another one of my favorite things on RAGBRAI.) A ball cap works just fine when I'm not wearing my bike helmet.

Right now matters.

Our goal on each year's ride is to visit as many children's lemonade or food stands on the route as possible. We love to support and encourage young entrepreneurs. As we pulled into one of the overnight towns on the 2019 ride, we stopped by one of those stands. A little girl was selling chocolate chip cookies and friendship bracelets. A fun combination, wouldn't you say? Well, I have a hard time resisting a good chocolate chip cookie, so we purchased both—a bag of cookies and a bracelet. I asked the little girl to pick out her favorite bracelet for me, and excitedly, she picked up a fuchsia, orange, and yellow braided one. I loved it! I held out my left arm, and her big sister tied it around my wrist. It was perfect. (And the cookies were wonderful too.)

As we hopped back on the bike and made our way to the campsite for the night, I remember looking at my left wrist. It was one of those moments where I marked time. This wasn't going to be just any old bracelet. It wasn't going to be something I threw away after the ride. This bracelet was going to mean something. It was going to stand for something. I desired for this bracelet to be a reminder to live in the moment, to live in the right now. Every time I looked at my left wrist, I wanted it to bring my thoughts to the present moment. This became a beautiful life-giving habit. As of this writing, I still wear that bracelet on my left wrist today. I don't take it off. It continually reminds me that right now matters. That bracelet is one simple thing that impacts my focus on a daily basis. I think of that little girl often and pray for her. She has no idea what a gift she gave me.

It is no secret we live in a culture of distraction, but it's time we make the most of it and choose to stop living distracted. It's time we embrace each moment we're given to live in God's grace and abundance. We will never receive this opportunity to live this day or this moment again. So let's not wait one minute longer because this moment is a priceless and wonderful gift. Let's tear it open. Together.

Lord, help us to appreciate the gift of each moment, Your priceless and wonderful gift. Right now matters to You, and it matters to us, too. Thank You. Amen.

[PAUSE]

Take a deep breath and pause. Bring your thoughts from wherever they are back to this present moment. Write out what impacted you in this chapter and anything you're noticing.

_____

_____

_____

_____

_____

_____

[PONDER]

Reflect on any ways you've lost sight of the importance of right now. Write down what comes to your mind.

_____

_____

_____

_____

_____

_____

[PRAY]

Ask God to help give your complete attention to what He is doing in your life right now. Ask Him to help you live in each moment of today, fully aware of His presence. Write it out here.

_____

_____

_____

_____

_____

_____

[PRAISE]

Thank and praise God throughout your day for the many blessings you notice.

_____

_____

_____

_____

_____

_____

2

THERE'S GOT TO BE MORE

What if we focus on living our lives abundantly?

L ike most new brides, I was on cloud nine—except on Sunday evenings. Being married less than a year, on Sunday evenings my thoughts would invariably turn to the following morning with dread and apprehension. I didn't like Mondays because I didn't like returning to my job. Don't get me wrong, I was thankful for my job. It was unheard of for someone as young as me without proper credentials to have the job I held. I worked at a great company with amazing people, and some are still my friends today. I was tremendously grateful, but secretly, I was also miserable. My job wasn't fulfilling. It was good, but it wasn't meaningful. And I remember specifically thinking as I drove to work most days, *there's got to be more to life than this.*

My job was distracting me from the life I desired to live. I had this deep desire to work for myself and own my own business. I felt as if I had this big "thing" inside of me that was just waiting to get out. Maybe it was a dream or a hope or a passion I just couldn't pinpoint at the time. I understood this misery was likely for a reason, and somehow, I needed to make a change. But how? We needed the income and insurance. I couldn't just quit with no other options. That wasn't a realistic choice for us.

I find it interesting what can happen when we invite God into our situations. When we ask God for direction, for guidance, for His will in our lives, He may answer in ways we couldn't dream of or expect. He answered my prayer for my there's-got-to-be-more declaration with a pregnancy and an at-home business.

So when our daughter was born, I left that job to raise her and her brother (born three years later), and to run my own business.

There's got to be more to life than this. Countless women daily consider similar thoughts, maybe for different reasons than I did. Maybe you are even one of them. I hear their desperate pleas. I see their anxious faces. I feel the heaviness in their hearts, and I understand their desire for more in this life.

Distractions aren't just something to avoid to make our lives more enjoyable; they are something to avoid to make our lives more impactful.

Every day we experience an onslaught of distractions attempting to entice us away from God's good plans and purposes for our lives. And when we give in to those distractions, when we let them rule and run us, we feel a gaping hole inside. We know something is missing, something we can't quite put our fingers on or figure out. Before we know it, those distractions have moved us farther away from God's will for our lives. These everyday distractions can be persuasive tools our spiritual enemy uses against us to lure us into being unproductive and ineffective in life.

We're warned in 1 Peter 5:8 to stay alert and to watch out for this great enemy, the devil, for he "prowls around like a roaring lion, looking for someone to devour." Friend, he wants to devour us. And one sneaky way he can do that is to distract us. He knows how to affect and manipulate us, for he sees our tendencies and recognizes what will hinder our growth and keep us from becoming the women God desires us to be. He will do all he can to keep us distracted and ineffective.

Craig Groeschel, founder and senior pastor of Life.Church once said,

> "Would you believe it if I told you that your spiritual enemy wants to separate your mind from focusing on the things of God, to separate your heart from living for what matters most? Every force in hell wants to distract you, to divide your heart, to discourage your soul, to disengage your faith. In fact, I would argue that the devil doesn't need to destroy you if he can distract you. If he can distract you, eventually over time you will destroy yourself. Your life is valuable. Your calling is great, and your enemy is real who wants to distract you. If he can't distract you by doing something bad, he'll just distract you by doing anything to keep you out of what God has created you to do."[5]

This lights a fire in me because this describes the seriousness of living distracted. This forces us to grapple with the reality of how destructive distractions can be in our lives. Distractions aren't just something to avoid to make our lives more enjoyable; they are something to avoid to make our lives more impactful. Distractions are robbing us of the abundant, joy-filled lives Jesus came to give us. I shared this verse in the last chapter, but let's take a look at it again.

"The thief approaches with *malicious intent*, looking to steal, slaughter, and destroy; I came to give life with joy and abundance" (John 10:10 Voice).

To clarify, not every distraction we experience originates with this spiritual enemy. For example, if a loved one calls and needs my attention, that interruption may be a distraction, but it's also an opportunity to be present and available to the one who needs me. Instead, the kinds of distractions I'm referring to draw us away from what God desires for us and what He calls us to do. They lure us away to less meaningful and less important matters. If we're focused on what's less important, we can't think about, let alone pursue, what's life-changing and life-impacting. Bottom line: these distractions make us ineffective. They steal, slaughter, and destroy our hopes, plans, and good intentions—our very lives! This makes me want to stand up and do all I can to overcome these distractions and help other women do the same.

I'm tired of this enemy robbing me of life. Robbing others of life. Stealing dreams. Ripping apart goals. Destroying the present moment through this culture of distraction. This is one reason I help women live encouraged and undistracted. I want women to experience the freedom of living in the moment. I desire for them to embrace the gift of right now and not be concerned with the past or the future. I long for them to be able to focus on what really matters in life, so they—women like you and me—can impact this world for good—and for God. I pray women would never feel the need to think or utter those dreadful words again, *there's got to be more to life than this.*

Right now matters.

But we often don't even realize we are distracted. We just know we are miserable. Our attention is all over the place, and we cannot stay focused no matter how hard we try. We desire more in our lives—more abundance, peace, joy, hope, but feel as if life is swallowing us whole. We do not realize distractions are running and ruining our lives. I had a recent conversation with someone who confirmed these thoughts. She shared, "I had no idea I was living so distracted until I saw you talking about it on social media. I felt my life was spinning out of control, and now I know why. I'm taking my life back from these distractions." Amen, sister! Does this resonate with you, too?

When we live distracted, we miss what's important in life.

Don't skim over that. We've traded the simple, uncomplicated life for the frenzied, distracted life. Adam Gazzaley and Larry D. Rosen in their book, *The Distracted Mind: Ancient Brains in a High-Tech World*, offer this observation:

When we live distracted, we miss what's important in life.

"This noise [interference from distractions] degrades our perceptions, influences our language, hinders effective decision making, and derails our ability to capture and

recall detailed memories of life events. ... People do not sit and enjoy a meal with friends and family without checking their phones constantly. We no longer stand idle in waiting lines, immersed in thought or interacting with those next to us. Instead, we stare face down into virtual worlds beckoning us through our smartphones. We find ourselves dividing our limited attention across complex demands that often deserve sustained, singular focus and deeper thought."[6]

In other words, distracted living negatively impacts our quality of life.

When we live distracted, we lose our sense of focus, purpose, and direction. When that happens, our minds get confused and we detach mentally, causing us to become almost intellectually paralyzed, not knowing what to do or which direction to go next. These distractions have such a hold on us we give in to them day after day. In fact, it's easier to give in to them than to fight them. Yet some of us don't realize these distractions are affecting us so negatively. We cannot see beyond the distractions. We become numb in life, forgetting the hope and promise that's now buried under the rubble deep within our hearts.

There's got to be more to life than this. Friend, there is.

Are you living distracted? How do you know? Here are a few indications. You may be living distracted if:

- **You have a difficult time staying focused**. At work, at home, behind the wheel, or out with friends, do you find your mind wandering away often? Do you catch yourself thinking about something else instead of what you're doing in the moment? Are your thoughts scattered much of the time? Have you ever driven to your destination, but you don't completely remember driving there? If you answered yes to any of these, it's a good indication you might be living distracted.

- **You find it challenging to complete tasks in a timely manner.** If you're anything like me, your to-do list or task list can be quite long some days, and it feels like it's a race against the clock to cross everything off. Do you often find you aren't able to complete what you need to get done? What stops you from completing the tasks and crossing them off? Is it other people or issues that pop up? Is it your own mind wandering? Is it your notifications dinging? If you continue to move your task list to the next day, you may be living distracted.

- **You often find yourself in a rush.** This can be a clue you may be living distracted. Because the more distracted we are living, the more we will feel the need to rush. Distractions make us feel like we are consistently behind. But rushing is a distraction itself. We miss what's going on around us when we rush. This may be the one I struggle with the most. Most days I must intentionally slow myself down because my natural pace is hurried. If you're often rushing, it's wise to pause and ask, "Why do I feel the need to rush today? Why am I in such a hurry?"

- **You've lost your joy and peace.** This is another telltale sign of distracted living. Many of us don't even realize we've lost our joy and peace. We just keep doing what we're doing, not paying attention to the joy and peace (or lack thereof) we have on a daily basis. Let's do a check right now. On a scale of 1 to 10, with 1 being the lowest and 10 being the highest, how much joy do you have in life right now? (Remember, joy isn't dependent on our circumstances.) How much peace do you have in your life right now? If one or both are low, it's a good indication you may be living distracted. Distractions have a way of robbing us of our joy and our peace.

- **It's nearly impossible for you to enjoy the moment.** When you're with your friends or family, are you able to enjoy their company? Or are your thoughts taking you away from the moment? Can you sit for more than a short while, soaking in what's around you? Or is your mind filled with what's next on your list? Do you have a difficult time appreciating this precise moment, the sights, smells, tastes, and feelings associated with the reality around you? This is another challenging one for many of us, including me. It's not easy for me to sit and be still. I often feel I need to do something, think of what's ahead, or plan my next step. This is a good clue we may be living distracted.

If any of these describe you, please know you're in good company. Plenty of us can relate. But you and I have hope! The first step in undistracting our lives is to become aware. Well done! You've already taken the first step. We will explore the next steps in the coming chapters. You are not alone in this endeavor. I'm with you and so is our ever-present God. Living in the moment is His best for us, and He will guide us as we go.

"Be very careful, then, how you live—not as unwise but as wise, making the most of every opportunity, because the days are evil" (Ephesians 5:15-16).

We are to walk in wisdom and make the most of every moment. Every moment. Not just the big ones or the special ones. Not even just the good ones. Every moment.

This reminds me of the account of Mary and Martha in the Bible. It's found in Luke 10:38-42. Martha is distracted, but Mary is not. When Martha asks Jesus to tell Mary to help her, she suggests in her own way, "There's got to be more to life than this." Jesus' reply points us to how and why there *is* more to life than this. Here's what Luke detailed:

> *"As Jesus and his disciples were on their way, he came to a village where a woman named Martha opened her home to him. She had a sister called Mary, who sat at the Lord's feet listening to what he said. But Martha was distracted by all the preparations that had to be made. She came to him and asked, 'Lord, don't you care that my sister has left me to do the work by myself? Tell her to help me!'*
>
> *'Martha, Martha,' the Lord answered, 'you are worried and upset about many things, but few things are needed—or indeed only one. Mary has chosen what is better, and it will not be taken away from her.'"*
>
> —Luke 10:38-42

Did you catch "...but few things are needed—or indeed only one" (Luke 10:42a)? One thing. What is that one thing? Mary chose to sit at the feet of Jesus, learn from Him, and spend time with Him. Mary's priority was Jesus. Martha's priority was hospitality and dinner.

How do we apply this story? You and I have work to do, like Martha, but we also want to learn from Jesus, like Mary. I don't want to discount Martha's role and her response here and only praise Mary for hers. I'm guessing this is a struggle for both of us. We want to be like Mary, yet have responsibilities like Martha.

Jesus is always what's better.

But I wonder, if Jesus came to my house today, what would my priority be? I want to be like Mary, but I think I might end up being more like Martha. I would want everything to be perfect for Jesus. He deserves the best, doesn't He? But clearly, as He states in this text, that's not what He desires. That's not what He considers the one thing needed and what was better. Jesus is always what's better.

Often, I make other things the better things, and I can frequently be distracted away from the "one thing" needed. The Message paraphrase of verse 40 says that Martha was "pulled away by all she had to do in the kitchen" (Luke 10:40 MSG). How often am I "pulled away" from what's important to something less important? How often do I put other things ahead of what is better? Do you do this, too? And what lures me away from choosing what's better? Distractions. Those pesky, sometimes all-consuming distractions.

Mary found the answer to this dilemma: "There's got to be more to life than this." She figured it out. I pray we do too.

Lord, help us be wise and to make the most of every moment. Guide us, equip us, and help us to live the abundant lives Jesus came to give us. Amen.

[PAUSE]

Take a deep breath and pause. Bring your thoughts from wherever they are back to this present moment. Write what impacted you in this chapter and anything you're noticing right now.

_____

_____

_____

_____

_____

_____

_____

[PONDER]

Reflect on the five signs listed toward the end of this chapter to become aware if you are living distracted. Write down anything that stands out to you.

_____

_____

_____

_____

_____

_____

[PRAY]

Ask God to reveal to you what is most commonly distracting you and when you most consistently fall into distractions. Sit quietly and pay attention to anything He shows you. Write it out here.

_____

_____

_____

_____

_____

_____

_____

[PRAISE]

Thank and praise God for any revelations or guidance He is giving you of how distractions are affecting you and your life.

_____

_____

_____

_____

_____

_____

_____

3

TOO BUSY TO NOTICE

What if we remove the word busy from our lives?

With sleep still clouding my eyes, I shuffled my way in those early morning hours to my coffee pot. The lovely aroma of fresh brewing coffee would soon not only permeate our home, but my senses as well. I anticipated the lingering trance of slumber to dissipate with that first sip. There's nothing like the first sip in the morning, am I right?

As I pressed the button to grind the coffee beans, something colorful caught my eye through our kitchen window. Gazing outward, I was stunned to see some of the most beautiful colors cascading across the horizon. Shades of amber mixed with coral and fuchsia graced the blue-backdrop sky, along with a few colors I might have never seen. The sun was nearing its morning rousing, ready to adorn the day with its presence, and the sight of it all was incredibly breathtaking. *Only God could create something this beautiful.*

As I stood there with my empty coffee cup in hand, I watched the colors morph and transform before my eyes. The hues changed with each passing second. The sky became more beautiful and vibrant. I didn't want to take my eyes off the sky and miss any of it. So I stayed right there, my eyes fixed. As the sun inched over the horizon, the colors faded, little by little. Standing there, I wondered how many sights like this I missed each morning as the sun made its grand appearance. I knew I did not want to miss another one. Isn't it interesting how one experience can impact your life forever? This was that kind of experience for me. My mornings would never again be the same.

The rising sun wasn't something I typically paid attention to. Although it takes place every day, I had never noticed how or when the sun crested over the horizon. It just did without my observation or care about it—until that morning. My heart swelled with gratitude in those moments standing in front of our kitchen window and I began to question, *Why me? Why right now? Why am I blessed to behold such a sight?* This led me to more questions. *Did God paint this sky just for me? God, what are You trying to tell me? How many other amazing sunrises had I missed over the years because I was too busy to notice?*

Too busy to notice. That was me in every sense. I didn't like being so busy. I didn't care for the pace of my life because it was all too much and too fast. But I figured that's just the way my life was since that's really all I knew. My life was jam-packed. Activity consumed my daily routine of raising a teenager and young adult with my husband, to running a business and working part-time in ministry. I also managed our home and tried to write when I could. In order to keep the balls in the air and successfully juggle my activities, busyness became the story of my life. It just had to be that way; if it wasn't, I would drown. Or so I thought. I would soon find out God had another pace in mind for me—one that was less busy and less distracted.

It's no wonder distractions were consuming my life, similar to those that ripped my attention from my son's incredible soccer play. I was missing out on living in the present because of my distracted life, and frankly, I was tired of it. There had to be a better way to live, but how? How does one just stop living distracted in a culture that embraces it? I knew I needed help, and I needed it now.

I had been praying for God to align my thoughts with His to keep me present and help me live in His ways, not buried under the distractions of my life. I knew His ways were better for me than the ways I was living, and I knew God had the answers. He could handle what I could not.

When I find myself struggling with something, I like to define what I'm struggling with. To help my understanding, I will search for definitions of correlating words. So I looked up the word "distract" which means "to draw away or divert, as the mind or attention; to disturb or trouble greatly in mind; beset."[7] Synonyms of distract are "fluster; mislead; perplex; bewilder; confound; unbalance."[8] No wonder I was struggling. These words described exactly how I felt living distracted. Especially that last word: unbalanced.

That's what distracted living does for us. It causes us to be unbalanced. It bewilders and confounds us because we don't like living this way, and we weren't designed to. We want to be present and live in the moment, but we've somehow allowed distractions to overrun and overrule our lives. Distractions are sneaky. They don't overtake us all at once, but slowly lure and entice us, one small step at a time until we are completely engulfed by them. Yet some of us are so accustomed to living in this manner, it doesn't even cross our minds to make a change. We've just accepted *this is how my life is, and that's the way it's going to be.* Some of us might not even realize we are living this way. Some of us are unaware how far the distractions have lured us off the path of the engaged life we once traveled. Because we've lived distracted for so long, we forget there's another—and better—way to live.

Because we've lived distracted for so long, we forget there's another—and better—way to live.

But this isn't God's best for us. God desires for us to live in His abundance daily. Living distracted is not His design for our lives. "Many are the plans in a person's heart, but it is the Lord's purpose that prevails" (Proverbs 19:21).

His plans and purposes for our lives are good, and they don't include living distracted. When in Scripture do we ever see Jesus distracted? I can't find a single example. He was always focused, in tune with the Father, and never wasted a moment or an opportunity.

Because of this truth, I knew there had to be a way to break the chains of distraction. I also knew I couldn't do it on my own. Numerous times I tried and failed miserably. The hold these distractions had on me was stronger than I was.

Still standing there in awe as my coffee finished brewing that morning, the aroma brought me back to my kitchen. I poured the liquid joy into my coffee cup, took the first wonderful sip, and turned back to the kitchen window. The vibrant colors had faded by that time. All that remained were a few thin, almost transparent, clouds suspended in the sky with the sun slowly climbing higher through them.

As it gradually ascended, I was reminded of how God not only created the sun and the moon, but God created this day as well, and He was already going before me. He already knew what was going to happen throughout the day. Still, I was privileged enough to pause in that moment and behold a glimpse of His handiwork as the sun rose over the horizon. It was almost as if I had watched Him create the gift of that day, wrapped in those beautiful God-painted colors that splashed across the sky. Just for me. Just for us.

I suddenly longed for a similar experience every morning. Instead of hurriedly making my coffee and rushing through the morning, I wanted an intentional, slower-paced, less-distracting start to my day. I desired this "appointment" with God every morning. Just us and the sunrise. Was God using His sunrises to slow me down, refocus me, and draw me to Him? If this was His plan, it was working.

I no longer desired to be too busy to notice.

From that day on, sunrises became something incredibly special to me. Not only are they my morning "appointments" with God, but they remind me to stay focused and remain present as I take them in each day. They help bring me back to the moment since I intentionally set my focus on what I see. My mind doesn't wander because most mornings I am awestruck watching the various colors and the sun fill the eastern sky.

Sunrises aren't just breathtakingly beautiful, they also fill me with hope as I start my day. As I investigated this further, I found watching the sunrise is actually good for us. Researchers at the University of Washington Health Sciences say the wavelengths at sunrise and sunset have the biggest impact on our brain centers that regulate our circadian (internal) clocks, our mood, and our alertness.[9] So watching the sunrise helps us sleep, helps us with positivity and happiness, and aids us in staying alert throughout the day. It also blesses us with vitamin D if we step outside and watch the sunrise, benefiting our health in all sorts of ways.

I once took these sunrises for granted; now I appreciate and behold them in an entirely new way. They are beautiful reminders of how

God is with me, no matter what's going on in my life. Yes, even on cloudy days. Although we can't see it, we know the sun still rises. The clouds may cover the sun, but we know it's still there. I guess that's kind of like faith, isn't it? Even though we cannot see it, we know the sun is shining brightly. Even though we may not see God with our eyes, we know He is with us. Hebrews 11:1 (NLT) says, "Faith shows the reality of what we hope for; it is the evidence of things we cannot see."

On the days when the sun isn't present, I'm reminded God is still present even if I don't see Him, feel Him, or experience Him. He is with me, and He is with you always. That is faith.

Before the colors faded that morning, I attempted to capture the scene. Still standing there in awe, I cranked open the window and extended my phone outside to snap a photo. I didn't want to forget those beautiful colors cascading across the morning sky. I had to re-member that life-changing morning.

Out here in rural Iowa, we live in a wide-open space. Our closest neighbor is a quarter mile away, so I guess some would say we live "in the middle of nowhere." From our home, we can see quite a distance in every direction, except for a small crest of a hill which blocks our south view. We are able to view the sun rising in the east and setting in the west. Since that infamous sunrise morning, I have snapped hundreds of photos of sunrises and sunsets from our home. Taking photos of the sun rising and setting has become almost a daily ritual for me. Some days, even in my pajamas, even when snow covers our Iowa ground, I'll slip on my boots and coat and step outside to pho-tograph the sunrise. If you follow me on social media, you've likely witnessed these God-painted sunrises and sunsets through my posts.

Living too busy is not God's best for us, nor His design for our lives.

God can use anything to help refocus us. For me, He uses sunrises. What does He use for you? If you're unsure, pay attention to what slows you down over the next week. Notice what makes you pause and take a second look. Like the sunrise did for me that morning, sometimes God grabs our attention with what we least expect. Sometimes He uses the simplest reminder to slow us down and bring us back to reality so He can begin the process of undistracting our lives.

May we not be too busy to notice.

Living too busy is not God's best for us, nor His design for our lives. When we're too busy in life, we're too busy to notice God's daily presence and blessings. Being busy isn't necessarily a bad thing unless it consumes our lives and controls our pace. That's when busyness snatches away our peace and leads us to a barren place called burnout.

It may help to keep these in perspective:

- Busy is not a badge of honor.
- Busy is an unhealthy rush many are addicted to.
- If we are too busy to do what we enjoy, then we're too busy.
- Our priorities determine what we do. We choose our busy.
- Living a too-busy life leads to an empty life.
- Busy doesn't mean better.

- Being busy and being productive are not the same.

- We learn something when we are too busy: that we don't like it.

As I mentioned, there's nothing wrong with being busy. For numerous years I was the recipient of business and leadership training from Mary Kay Ash, founder of Mary Kay, Inc. Her wisdom was worth heeding, and I remember she would often say, "Busy people get the most done." I agree. You and I get more done when we're active and on the go. We prioritize, we are engaged, and we are attentive. We tend to accomplish more when we're busy.

But what *are* we getting done? Are we being busy for the sake of being busy? Have we overcommitted ourselves and have too much in our schedules? What exactly is keeping us busy?

Living too busy causes us to live distracted. Like the time I forgot to pick up a child at school. (Okay, truth be told, I did that more than once.) Or the time I wore two different earrings without noticing until I looked in my rearview mirror on the way home from work. Then there was the time I forgot important information like the death of a family member's dog only to ask about the dog in a conversation. This caused my family member's eyes to well up with tears, and I felt like an insensitive and uncaring person. Oh, and the time I missed my exit on the highway, which added thirty miles to my trip! I did that more than once on the same exit—just different trips. Good grief!

Right now is the perfect time to hop off the hamster wheel and stop this madness. We all know how hamster wheels work. The hamster runs and runs on its wheel, but he gets nowhere. I used to be that hamster, running but getting nowhere until I eventually fell off. Maybe you can relate? It's time for us to stop being too busy to notice before we fall off the wheel and hurt ourselves—or others.

One simple step I took in refusing to be too busy was removing the word "busy" from my vocabulary. I know this may seem weird or insignificant, but let me tell you, this was no easy task. Busy was such a way of life for me; the word permeated my language. But I kept at it and decided to replace it with the word "full." Instead of saying, "I have a busy life," I now say, "I have a full life."

The word "busy" is defined as "full or characterized by activity."[10] Some synonyms are: "bustling; hectic; restless; tiring."[11] Whereas, the word "full" means "as completely filled; filled to almost capacity,"[12] and synonyms include "abundant; adequate; and sufficient."[13]

I like "full" so much better.

Even writing the word *busy* numerous times in this chapter is making me uncomfortable because it really is a word I no longer say. So, if you're looking for a simple way to hop off the busyness hamster wheel, removing the word *busy* from your vocabulary is a good first step.

How much are we missing when we're too busy to notice?

How much are we missing when we're too busy to notice? For me—for countless years—maybe it was the morning sunrise or the sunset. Maybe it's our neighbor's wave from across the street or the bird flitting in the bird bath in our back yard. Could it be we're missing the lush green grass under our feet or the face of a fellow man or woman who could use an encouraging smile? Could we be missing something important or valuable, something God wants to teach us or a way He wants to bless us? Are we missing out on life because we're too busy to notice?

I pray we aren't. Right now is a good moment to take inventory on how we're living, how busy we are, and what exactly is making us busy. Living too busy causes us to live distracted, but let's choose to live differently today. Let's choose to live differently right now.

Right now matters.

Lord, show us how to remove the busy from our lives and live undistracted. We don't want to miss one single thing You have for us. Amen.

[PAUSE]

Take a deep breath and pause. Bring your thoughts from wherever they are back to this present moment. Write out what impacted you in this chapter and anything you're noticing right now.

_____

_____

_____

_____

_____

_____

[PONDER]

Think about what fills your days. What are you busy doing? How are you too busy to notice God's blessings around you? Where do you need to make a change? Write what comes to mind.

_____

_____

_____

_____

_____

_____

[PRAY]

Seek God's best for you by asking Him to reveal how you can live less busy to become undistracted. Ask Him to align your daily schedule with His perfect plans and purposes for your life. Write your prayer here.

_____

_____

_____

_____

_____

_____

[PRAISE]

Thank and praise God for any truth He is revealing to you and for any changes He is prompting you to make.

_____

_____

_____

_____

_____

_____

4

DISTRACTIONS EVERYWHERE

*What if we address our distractions
to overcome them?*

We're not the only ones who are distracted. Every age and every culture has dealt with and will deal with distractions. Even those in biblical times:

- David was distracted by Bathsheba (2 Samuel 11).

- Sarai (Sarah) was distracted by the desire for a son (Genesis 16).

- Martha was distracted by good activities (Luke 10:38-42).

- Eve was distracted by temptations and the serpent (Genesis 3:1-7).

- Peter was distracted by the wind and the waves (Matthew 14:25-30).

- Samson was distracted by Delilah (Judges 16).

- The Israelites were distracted by their past (Exodus 16).

These examples give me comfort, knowing great people in the Bible were distracted too. It's not just us, but many who struggle with this! Today, just like in biblical times, the distractions are varied and plenty. Look at all the different examples of distractions: other people, personal desires, good activities, temptation and evil, the environment, and the past. We still have those same distractions affecting us today. Yet we also see examples of numerous people in the Bible who lived undistracted. We'll discuss a handful of them in Chapter 10.

For now, let's pause and appreciate where we are. We're realizing, maybe for the first time, how distractions are plaguing us and pulling us away from the abundant lives Jesus came to give us. We know there's got to be more than how we've been living. We're ready to learn how to overcome these distractions to free ourselves from their grip and take back our lives. We're ready to embrace the undistracted life!

I'm excited about where we are and what's ahead for us, aren't you? But before we can focus on overcoming distractions, we must understand what is distracting us in the first place. What is hijacking our attention? What is snatching us away from the present moment? These distractions don't just pop up once a day, but they can bombard us all day long, sometimes before we put our feet to the floor in the morning. They drop in and invade our minds when we least expect them. We may not even be aware of them until we walk into a room and forget what we came there to do. Or we can't remember where we put the TV remote. Or we don't remember if we turned off the burner after making our morning tea and leaving the house. (Am I the only one?)

If we pause to recall the numerous distractions we face on any given day, we might tally a long list—too many to even recount. For context, I jotted down some of the distractions I faced while writing this chapter. Here they are:

- my buzzing phone (*Hmm, who is texting me? I better check.*)

- my random, wandering thoughts (*What should we have for dinner? What will I wear to my speaking engagement on Sunday? How is my friend... maybe I should call her?*)

- my growling stomach (*I should eat!*)

- my incoming emails (*I better respond to these.*)

- our outside farm cat meowing (*What's up with him?*)

- my cluttered desk (*I should clean this right now.*)

Sadly, these were just in the last hour. Seriously. It's nearly impossible to count every distraction we face in a day.

For the sake of clarity and simplicity, let's lump distractions into two major categories: 1) external; and 2) internal. Adam Gazzaley and Larry D. Rosen, coauthors of *The Distracted Mind, Ancient Brains in a High-Tech World*, explain it this way, "Distractions are pieces of goal-irrelevant information that we either encounter in our external surroundings or generate internally within our own minds."[14]

External distractions originate from what's happening around us. For example, our phones and their notifications, music playing in the next room, an unexpected visitor, or a cluttered space. Internal distractions, on the other hand, originate within us and cause us to lose our focus. This is sometimes referred to as "mind wandering," such as thinking about the next thing on our to-do list as we converse with a coworker. Or remembering while making lunch that we forgot to call a friend on her birthday three days ago. Or while reading a bedtime story to our children, we find ourselves mentally replaying and reliving a mistake we made last week. A Harvard study found that we spend nearly 47% of our waking hours in this kind of mind wandering or thinking about something other than what we are doing at the moment.[15] That's startling, isn't it? Our thoughts are elsewhere almost half of the time.

So what is distracting you the most? Are your distractions external or internal? Do they exist in your environment or originate from within you? Maybe you're not sure because you have never taken the time to analyze them. Here's your chance. I invite you to pause and take five minutes to think about what distracted you in the last twenty-four hours, and also what distracted you in the past week. Don't miss this activity. This is a key step. List them here:

_____

_____

_____

_____

_____

_____

_____

_____

_____

Are they external, internal, or both? For example, the farm cat meowing outside my window is an external distraction, but my thought about what to make for dinner is internal. I seem to have a plentiful mix of both daily. You probably do too.

In the process of writing this chapter, I asked women through an online questionnaire to share their distractions. I already knew my typical distractions, but this questionnaire and their answers confirmed the real-life distractions women face, and it helped me realize we are all in this together. I'm grateful for the five minutes they took to be honest and open in their responses.

The first two questions I asked were the same questions you just answered: **What distracted you in the last twenty-four hours, and what distracted you in the past week?** Every single answer had a mixture of both external and internal distractions.

The results are below. I grouped their answers together according to commonality. Put a check mark next to the ones similar to your list.

ENVIRONMENT/SURROUNDINGS

- ◻ my cluttered space

- ◻ my messy house

- ◻ ridiculous amounts of snow/unfavorable weather

REAL-LIFE CIRCUMSTANCES:

- ◻ my life struggles

- ◻ lack of finances

- ◻ difficult family relationships

- ◻ challenging work duties

- ◻ my never-ending to-do list

- ◻ losing something important

- ◻ my disorganization

- ◻ varied responsibilities fighting for attention

- ◻ lack of time to complete all I need to finish

- ◻ family member's illness

WORLD/HEADLINES/EVIL:

- unsettling news headlines
- the condition of this world
- our spiritual enemy, his ways, and how he affects me
- divisiveness in the world

PHONES/DEVICES/NOTIFICATIONS:

- phone calls and text interruptions
- texting while driving (*gah!*)
- emails
- playing digital games

SOCIAL MEDIA

- enticement to scroll through social media feeds
- wasting time on social media
- the time it takes to post/interact on social media
- answering messages on social media

TV/MUSIC:

- listening to music
- staying up too late at night to finish a show
- binge watching TV
- watching the morning weather only to still be in front of the TV an hour later
- hearing the TV in the other room while trying to focus on something else

PEOPLE/PETS:

- coworkers' interruptions
- family members and their needs
- pets' needs
- spontaneous conversations with others
- my responsibility to care for those who rely on me

Can you relate to any of these? How many are similar to what is on your list? How many check marks did you add? The number of external distractions is great.

Now for the internal distractions that affected those who participated in my questionnaire:

ATTITUDES/EMOTIONS/FEELINGS:

- fear of the future
- sadness
- joy
- excitement
- feeling constantly overwhelmed
- fear
- worry (about numerous things!)
- regrets of my past
- feeling inadequate
- falling in love

THOUGHTS/DAYDREAMING:

- unhealthy/unhelpful thoughts

- sad memories

- fun memories

- my busy mind

- making decisions and pondering upcoming ones

- thinking of my kids

- missing my grandchildren

- thinking about what to make for dinner (*I guess I'm not the only one distracted by this!*)

- random thoughts

- planning

- figuring out logistics

- daydreaming about the future

- wondering where God is in my life

- new ideas/brainstorming

- looking forward to something

HEALTH:

- physical pain

- insomnia

- challenging health issues

- fatigue

COMPARISON/COMPETITION:

- wondering why others succeed and I don't
- caring about what other people think of me
- focusing on pleasing others
- trying to keep up with others

MULTITASKING:

- while working on one thing, I see another thing I need to do
- attempting to do too much at once
- my schedule is full, so I'm trying to do it all but can't

Can you relate to any of these internal distractions? Are any similar to what's on your list? How many check marks did you add? Some days the internal distractions bother me more than external ones.

Which in either list stands out to you the most? Something I noticed, and maybe you did too, is not all distractions are negative. Some are good things in our lives, such as falling in love, fun memories, and excitement. This leads us to the reality that not all distractions are bad. We'll discuss more of that truth in Chapter 11.

The percentage of external versus internal distractions in this questionnaire surprised me. External distractions were 59% and internal ones were 41%. I guess I expected internal distractions to be a greater number because, as I mentioned, those bother me the most. But considering the varied and numerous external distractions these women listed, it's no wonder the external distraction percentage was greater.

What excites me most is their answers to the next question. I asked them to share something they already do to overcome distractions.

Here are several of their answers:

- "Pray, read my Bible, memorize scriptures, journal thoughts, worship."

- "I removed a social media app from my phone this week."

- "I remind myself Jesus allowed Himself to be interruptible, and I can too."

- "Set a schedule."

- "Redirect myself."

- "I'm learning how to manage my mind."

- "Exercise and deep breathing to redirect myself."

- "To stay focused, I write a to-do list for each day."

- "I put my phone aside and try to be intentional about what I'm doing in the moment. If I'm doing laundry, I finish it before I sit down at my computer, etc. I think being a multitasker is what keeps me distracted."

- "Ask God for help."

- "Make to-do lists."

- "Set a timer to work on a project for forty minutes, and don't answer the phone during that time."

- "Plan ahead."

- "Set times for checking email."

- "Try to catch myself and reroute."

- "Stop, put some peaceful music on, and close my eyes."

- "Being intentional with my time helps me focus."

Wow. I'm impressed! These are all fantastic ways to overcome distractions. Do any of these stand out to you? Which ones would you like to implement? Is another idea coming to your mind right now? Write them down to remember later:

_____

_____

_____

_____

_____

_____

_____

What is something you currently do to overcome the distractions in your life? List it here:

_____

_____

_____

_____

_____

_____

These tips from those who answered my questionnaire are great starting points. In the chapters ahead, however, we are stepping into brave territory. We discover how to overcome these distractions to live an abundant, undistracted life. We learn how to apply helpful tools I've either taught myself or learned along the way to embrace this new way of undistracted living. Let's step forward together.

Right now matters.

> *Lord, thank You for helping us become aware of distractions in our lives. We realize living distracted is not Your best for us. Please continue to guide us. Amen.*

[PAUSE]

Take a deep breath and pause. Bring your thoughts from wherever they are back to this present moment. Write what you're noticing right now.

_____

_____

_____

_____

_____

_____

[PONDER]

Reflect on your answers of what distracts you, and think about how they are pulling you away from reality and God's best for your life. Write down anything that comes to your mind.

_____

_____

_____

_____

_____

_____

[PRAY]

Ask God to help you take the next step in overcoming the distractions in your life. Write out your prayer here.

_____

_____

_____

_____

_____

_____

[PRAISE]

Thank and praise God for any revelations or guidance He is giving you, and for making you aware of how distractions are affecting your life.

_____

_____

_____

_____

_____

_____

5

THE BIG FIVE

*What if we understand living
distracted is not what's best for us?*

As we discussed in the last chapter, it's nearly impossible to list the countless distractions we face on any given day. However, five distractions were common with those who answered the questionnaire from the last chapter. I call them the Big Five: the past, the future, technology, our thoughts, and multitasking. In this chapter we dive deeper into those five distractions for greater understanding why right now matters with each one.

THE PAST

We don't have to go back too far to think about the past because the past can be as short as a zeptosecond ago—a trillionth of a billionth of a second. It's a decimal point followed by twenty zeros and a one. That's short, huh?

When it comes to the past, an abundance of women do not like visiting it often. It's full of pain and mistakes and things we'd rather not remember. Yet some of us would return there right now if we could. Perhaps we feel it was better than what we're walking through today. Me? I have a love-hate relationship with my past. Maybe you do too. We have both good instances and not-so-good instances in our yesteryears. We hold fond memories from our pasts and also ones we'd rather forget. When you think of yours, what comes up first? The good stuff or the not-so-good stuff? Either way, this is where the distraction of the past enters the scene.

Today is a good old day because God is with us *today.*

The distraction of the past has two different facets: positive and negative. When the distraction of the past lures us from the present, we miss what's happening right here. The temptation to be pulled away may contain something positive from our past or something negative. Unfortunately, I've struggled with both sides.

We may think the good old days are only what we remember from the past. But this thought is missing something significant. The good old days aren't in the past. They are right here. Right now. *These* are the good old days—even if the past brings up fond memories and we carry them with us like a warm hug. Why is this? Because, as we discussed in Chapter 1, God is with us today. We'll look at this more in a minute, but today is a good old day. That's worth repeating. Today's goodness is not based on our circumstances, or the price of eggs, or the rapidly changing world, or the alarming headlines. Today is a good old day because God is with us today.

"Don't long for 'the good old days.' This is not wise" (Ecclesiastes 7:10 NLT).

The distraction of the past also draws us away from the present by bringing up negative experiences. And I've dealt with this more than I care to disclose here. Maybe you have too, and maybe you're stuck there today. I get it, and I'm sorry if you are. It's not a pleasant place to be stuck when the past isn't our friend. For a number of years I let my past sins, past mistakes, and past failures consume me. In a particular season of my life, I couldn't break free from it all. It consumed my reality. When I reflected on my mistakes and childish behavior, even as an adult, almost every thought I had was degrading or depleting. The *how-could-you* and the *you-will-never-rise-above-this* thoughts. The *mistakes-you-made-will-always-define-you* and the *you-are worthless-and-unworthy* thoughts.

Seems ironic, doesn't it? As one who speaks, writes, and hosts a podcast on encouragement; who finds her hope in Jesus; and who always tries to see the glass half-full, how could my inner voice have been so self-deprecating? But this distraction (like any distraction) doesn't play favorites. It can affect each one of us. That is one reason I'm passionate about helping women rise above these distractions. No one is immune to them, but we don't have to be stuck in them. We can learn to overcome them.

When prayer, reading God's Word, and focusing on changing my thoughts couldn't break me free from my past, I sought professional help. God crossed my path with a wonderful Christian therapist nearly five years ago. Through much hard work, consistent self-care, and guidance from God, my past no longer consumes my present. It no longer entices me away with those degrading and depleting thoughts.

Oh, but it still tries. However, I now possess the tools to "take captive every thought to make it obedient to Christ" (2 Corinthians 10:5). And I can now embrace the present to receive what God has for me, because I am no longer stuck in my past. And I don't want you to be stuck there either.

The past doesn't have to stop us from living in the present because that's not God's best for us. No matter if our thoughts regarding the past are positive or negative, this distraction keeps us stuck there. It coaxes us to rewind and relive what's already been, and that prevents us from living in the abundance of God today.

"Forget about what's happened; don't keep going over old history. Be alert, be present. I'm about to do something brand-new. It's bursting out! Don't you see it? There it is! I'm making a road through the desert, rivers in the badlands" (Isaiah 43:18-19 MSG).

Do you struggle with the distraction of the past? If so, how has this section prompted you to let go of the past and live in the moment?

THE FUTURE

I was recently reminded of a personal story about how the distraction of the future impacts our lives today, even as a twelve-year-old girl.

When I was a child, my mom shared that her mother died when she was twelve years old. In that conversation, something in my brain marked time. I wasn't quite twelve yet, but my simple mind led me to believe that if my mom's mom died when she was twelve, then my mom would likely die when I was twelve, on the anniversary of my grandmother's death.

It sounds a bit silly now that I'm an adult, but it wasn't silly to me back then. I mean, what child dwells on such awful thoughts? Well, this child did. Fear of the future impacted my thinking. My greatest fear back then was losing my mom, and that fear plagued me for years in my young life.

Well, eventually the anniversary of my grandmother's death arrived in my twelfth year of life, the day I thought I would lose my mom.

The future becomes a distraction when we allow fear and worry to fill it.

I was supposed to go with friends to an amusement park two hours away. But the thought of not being home with Mom that day nearly tore me apart. After her coaxing and comforting assurances, I went, eventually forgetting all about my fear and worry as I rode roller coasters, dined on cotton candy, and played arcade games. When I arrived home that evening, Mom met me at the door, and let me tell you, my young heart couldn't have been happier. All those years of fretting and worrying were for nothing.

Don't we do this as adults? We worry about things that will never happen. The future becomes a distraction when we allow fear and worry to fill it.

But that's not the only facet to the distraction of the future. The distraction of the future can also be a result of anticipating something good in our lives, like our hopes, dreams, or future goals and realities. Allow me to explain.

Have you ever dreamed about something specific in your future? Something wonderful or something you've desired for a long time? You put all your effort into it because you know when it's achieved, it'll be worth it. For years I worked with a company who awarded leased pink Cadillacs to their top performers, and I wanted to earn one. I planned and focused and worked until I finally achieved my goal. As I drove my pink Cadillac off the new car lot, I felt a great sense of accomplishment, but also an unexpected feeling of sadness.

I became acutely aware of how much this goal had distracted me from living my life in the present, all for the sake of achievement. All I could focus on was the future. All I could see was this goal. Now that I had achieved it, I questioned myself. *Was it all worth it?* Please don't get me wrong. I was thankful and appreciative, and I celebrated my hard work. But I also knew it came with a cost: missing the present life I was in to gain the life I wanted.

This distraction of the future entices us to fixate on what's to come. It snatches us away from what's happening right here and now and places our attention on a future we have no control over. The future that only God sees, knows, and controls. Whether it's a negative perspective of the future (with fear or worry) or a positive one (anticipating good things), we aren't designed to live in any space of time other than the current one.

"Give your entire attention to what God is doing right now, and don't get worked up about what may or may not happen tomorrow. God will help you deal with whatever hard things come up when the time comes" (Matthew 6:34 MSG).

God meets us in the present because we encounter Him in the present. Yes, God transcends time and is infinite, and He's the God of the past, present, and future. He's the same yesterday, today, and tomorrow. But He meets us right now. He gives us what we need in the present.

"Yes, we should make the most of what God gives, both the bounty and the capacity to enjoy it, accepting what's given and delighting in the work. It's God's gift! God deals out joy in the present, the *now*. It's useless to brood over how long we might live" (Ecclesiastes 5:19-20, MSG).

Do you struggle with the distraction of the future? If so, what's one step you can take today to live in the present instead?

Social media tempts us to spend time watching others live their lives instead of boldly living our own.

TECHNOLOGY

It's no secret our devices, social media, video games, and TV are big distractions in our lives these days. In my questionnaire, almost every woman responded with some form of technology as a distraction in her life. That's no surprise since 31% of adults now say they are "almost constantly" online.[16] Technology is an amazing tool, but have we given it too much control and access to our lives? Have we allowed it to become something we cannot live without?

The dings, the beeps, the buzzes. They all pull our attention away from what we're currently doing. Watching TV and playing video games can distract us and allow us to escape living our real lives. Social media tempts us to spend time watching others live their lives instead of boldly living our own.

Besides being a distraction, studies tell us technology can be quite addicting. We know that firsthand, don't we? This is our reality, even if we don't want to acknowledge it. Technology affects our attention, our mental health, and our relationships. It's stealing our time, our peace, and our sleep. It is overstimulating our brains, causing us to be less effective, and confounding our mental capacities. No wonder we're living distracted since this tool is within our grasp 24/7.

Either we rule over technology, or it rules over us. It's our choice!

However, technology is an external distraction we can control. We have complete authority over it. You and I can manage our phones and how long we're on them any given day. We are the ones to turn on the TV or the video games. We are the ones who choose to log in to our social media accounts, choose what we do on them, and choose how much access they have in our lives. It's up to us how much time we spend consuming and using technology. Either we rule over technology, or it rules over us. It's our choice!

I'm reminded of the words the apostle Paul wrote to the church at Corinth that may help us put this into perspective. These are words we can apply to the distraction of technology or to anything that has us in its grasp: "I can do anything I want to if Christ has not said no, but some of these things aren't good for me. Even if I am allowed to do them, I'll refuse to if I think they might get such a grip on me that I can't easily stop when I want to" (1 Corinthians 6:12 TLB).

Paul was specifically writing in regard to sexual immorality of that day, but his words also point us to truth in our times. He makes us aware how easy it is for us to be enticed and controlled by something other than what's good for us—by something other than God's presence and influence. Technology can be one of these enticements. It has a way of sneakily working its way into our lives to the point we wake up one day and believe we cannot live without it.

Now, I'm not indicating we are all addicted to technology, but if we find it difficult to be away from our phones, to set our gaming aside, or forget about technology or TV for a while, this might indicate technology has a bigger hold on us than we might have realized.

And we can do something about it. We can limit the access we allow technology to have in our everyday lives. We can take breaks from it periodically. You and I can turn them off (*gasp!*), and see how we feel "unconnected." My husband calls this "going acoustical," meaning going unplugged. Here's a fun test, if you're brave enough to try. Turn off your phone for the next hour and see how you feel. Do you feel relieved? Agitated? Peaceful? Completely stressed? Your feelings indicate how much or how little technology is impacting you and your life.

What's your biggest distraction when it comes to technology? What's one step you can take today to overcome it?

OUR THOUGHTS/OURSELVES

My friend said the other day, "I am my worst distraction." She shared how her thoughts wander. She can't seem to organize herself like she used to. She doesn't follow through on the things she wants or needs to. Having time to think—she calls it her "thinking time"—is important to her, yet she can't seem to ponder all her thoughts. She says, "There are just too many good and bad thoughts." I told her that I don't think she's her own worst distraction, but her thoughts might be.

Our thoughts can be one of our biggest internal distractions, and according to the answers from my questionnaire, you're not alone if your thoughts distract you. Here are some of the answers I received regarding our distracting thoughts:

- "I'm thinking about things I have to do that haven't been done yet."

- "My busy mind is always thinking about something."

- "I'm figuring out logistics."

- "I'm thinking through upcoming decisions and prioritizing the timeline of events."

- "I'm thinking of the kids."

- "I have random thoughts of other things that need to be done."

- "I'm easily distracted by random thoughts and new ideas I need to do in my business."

- "I'm planning future things."

- "I have thoughts and worries, particularly over relationships and finances."

- "I struggle with my own busy mind and my random thoughts."

- "I wonder what people think of me."

As we can see through these examples, our minds are full and our thoughts are all over the place some days, aren't they? We plan, we think, we ponder. We figure things out, we worry, we wonder. It makes sense how we can get distracted by our own brains!

As you read through these, can you relate to any? Are some of these similar to your own thoughts? Of course, not all thoughts are distractions—just the ones that try to lead us astray and rob us of the moment we're in, or the ones that cause us to think of something other than what we're doing.

Our thoughts are powerful. God knew what He was doing when He designed our brains. But I don't believe He desires our thoughts to become distractions. This is where we can choose our thoughts, and "think about such things" as Philippians 4:8 describes:

"Finally, brothers and sisters, whatever is true, whatever is noble, whatever is right, whatever is pure, whatever is lovely, whatever is admirable—if anything is excellent or praiseworthy—think about such things."

We can ask God to align our thoughts with His, and to help us think the thoughts He desires us to think. We don't have to entertain every thought that pops into our brains. As I say often, "We don't have to believe every thought we think."

When my mind races or when my thoughts seem random and all over the place, I take out my notebook and write down every thought that's running through my mind. I don't worry about complete sentences or punctuation or grammar. I just get my thoughts on paper and out of my head. Then, I often pray about what I wrote down, and I ask God to handle the things I can't control, then show me what to do with the rest. This exercise helps me regain control of my scattered thoughts. I invite you to give it a try and see how it helps. You may find it gives you clarity and discernment.

What consumes your thoughts? Are they distracting you from living right now? Is there some action you're prompted to take after reading this section?

We don't have to entertain every thought that pops into our brains.

MULTITASKING

Multitasking is defined as "computing the execution of various diverse tasks simultaneously; the carrying out of two or more tasks at the same time by one person."[17] An antonym of multitasking is "focus."[18] This speaks loudly: multitasking is the *opposite* of focus. And that is exactly what researchers today are saying. Our brains are not created to focus on more than one thing at a time.[19] In fact, it's impossible. Multitaskers believe that's what they are doing, when in reality, they are switching from one task to another very rapidly, even if it seems they are doing tasks simultaneously.

This constant switching back and forth taxes our brains and tires them out. Multitasking makes our brains less efficient, and it causes us to lose our focus, even when we aren't attempting to do more than one activity at a time. This makes me nervous. Friend, we can't go to the store and purchase another brain. You and I cannot get an upgraded version of the brains we currently possess. These are the brains God gave us, and it's wise to take care of them, don't you agree?

"One thing at a time" is a great motto to live by.

Multitasking can be a consuming distraction for me. Last week, I found myself struggling one afternoon while attending an online training, and I caught myself simultaneously creating a few social posts. As I listened to a voicemail, I realized I was also trying to skim an article. I was finishing my monthly tax prep, and at the same time,

I found myself scrolling on my phone. *Hello?* I was multitasking all afternoon. No wonder I was exhausted by the end of the day!

Multitasking causes us to make more errors and strains our brains more than when we focus on one task at a time. It's also less effective and more time consuming. Studies show multitasking takes as much as 40% more time to complete a task than doing one thing at a time.[20] As much as 40%! The verdict is still out on whether multitasking behaviors affect our brains in just the short term or the long term too. One study had participants memorize letters in sequence while also doing math problems. Interestingly, those who were frequent multitaskers in real life performed the worst, and the best performers were those who only multitasked sparingly in real life.

Multitasking is one of the biggest distractions in today's world for multiple reasons. One, we have more information than ever before bombarding our brains. We also have more on our plates and more in our schedules. We're doing the best we can with what we have, trying to live our best lives. But multitasking isn't the best for us. It's not God's best for us. If it were, He would have designed our brains to do more than one activity at a time. He would have equipped us to handle focusing on two things (or more) with ease. But He didn't. Because of this, I firmly believe He never meant for us to multitask.

"One thing at a time" is a great motto to live by. It's currently on my phone's lock screen as a reminder. Doing one thing at a time is less stressful, less time consuming, and much less distracting. Now knowing what we know about multitasking, doing one thing at a time is more efficient, and it is also better for our brains.

Do you struggle with multitasking? If so, a great first step is to consciously choose to perform one activity at a time. As with overcoming any distraction, it'll feel awkward and uncomfortable at first. But you can overcome multitasking. Just be patient with yourself.

Lord, thank You for equipping us to learn about these distractions and helping us to understand that living with these in our lives is not Your best for us. Help us to overcome them in Your power and strength. Amen.

[PAUSE]

Take a deep breath and pause. Right now, bring your thoughts from wherever they are back to this present moment. Write out what impacted you in this chapter and anything you're noticing.

_____

_____

_____

_____

_____

_____

[PONDER]

Reflect on these five distractions. Do you struggle with any of them? If so, which one is most frequent in your life? Write down how God is revealing these distractions to you and how they make you feel.

_____

_____

_____

_____

_____

[PRAY]

Ask God to help you take the next step in overcoming the distractions in your life, taking one step at a time. Write your prayer here.

_____

_____

_____

_____

_____

_____

_____

[PRAISE]

Thank and praise God for how He's guiding you and helping you see common distractions in your life.

_____

_____

_____

_____

_____

_____

_____

6

A DIFFERENT WAY

*What if we could overcome distractions
by partnering with God?*

A former pastor once shared wisdom with me that I've not forgotten: "You don't know what you don't know." His words weren't criticizing or condemning, but instead, he pointed to the reality that we do the best we can with what we know at the time. We apply the knowledge and wisdom we possess in the current moment. And until we learn something different, we just know what we know. Thankfully, we are always learning, growing, and maturing.

Up to this point, "we didn't know what we didn't know" about living distracted or how preoccupied we've been walking through our days. And "we didn't know what we didn't know" concerning the hope we have to overcome these distractions and live the abundant life Jesus came to give us. Friend, we are learning and growing! But we're not stopping there.

We are bravely stepping forward into the reality of how we can look these distractions straight in the eye and tell them they no longer have a place in our lives. We're done with letting them run and rule us. We have better things to do with our lives than to live them distracted.

We have better things to do with our lives than to live them distracted.

So here we go. This is the biggest secret to overcoming life's distractions: we cannot fight these distractions on our own. We just can't. We may think and believe we can, and self-help books may even say we can. Sure, we're capable, strong, and steadfast women. We are smart, talented, and skillful. You and I know how to get things done and how to make things happen, right? Common sense tells us we should be able to fight these distractions on our own. At least that's what we think, and that's likely what we desire.

My parents raised me to be an independent woman. I believe they knew me well enough to notice my independent tendencies as a young girl and fostered that trait in me. They showed me how to speak up for myself, yet they came to my rescue when I needed them. They encouraged me to try new things, which explains why I played every sport I possibly could in high school. My dad taught me how to drive a car and fill my car's gas tank. Mom taught me how to cook, sew, and do laundry, although I rarely did any of that until I was out on my own. I'm thankful they encouraged me to be independent without having to rely on anyone else to get by. They prepared me well to leave home and live on my own.

This, combined with the trait of stubbornness that has weaved its way through generations in my dad's lineage, created my confidence and pride in the fact I could do most anything on my own. You know how a two-year-old can be stubborn in wanting to do something without the help of an adult? That was me. Except I acted this way as a teenager and a young adult. *I do NOT need help, thank you very much.* This attitude wasn't the fault of my parents; it originated from my own pride and stubbornness.

So it's not always easy for me to do what our family terms "LG²," meaning, "Let Go and Let God." I know some people don't like this saying, but I think it's because they see it differently than I do. Our family says these five words as a reminder to relinquish control into God's hands. To trust Jesus to drive instead of trying to take the wheel ourselves. To follow God and His lead to forego our attempts to lead Him. (When has that ever worked out well?) This saying has helped lessen my grip on control and encouraged me to move over to the passenger seat, leaving the driving up to the One who is truly in charge. Let's just say God has certainly had His hands full when it comes to me.

I've learned on this journey of living undistracted that I am not strong enough to combat these distractions on my own. I need my Creator's help since no one knows me better than Him. In His power and strength I can live an undistracted life. On my own, I cannot. Not only this, but He knows the schemes of the evil one who comes to steal, kill, and destroy—the one who loves to distract us. No one is more powerful than God, including this enemy. *Who am I to think I can take on these distractions on my own?*

Here's the foundation of living an abundant life and overcoming distractions: we must partner with God. We must let Him lead, guide, and teach us what we need to know. Even if we're independent, self-sufficient women, it doesn't matter. We need God's help to equip us in living undistracted.

God is our Guide, our source, our strength. And He is the One who keeps us undistracted.

"Show me your ways, Lord, teach me your paths. Guide me in your truth and teach me, for you are God my Savior, and my hope is in you all day long" (Psalm 25:4-5).

I have prayed these two verses in this psalm so often, they are now cemented into my brain. As a side note, if you're ever not sure what to pray, I suggest praying Scripture. It's as simple as reading a Bible verse as a prayer or forming it into one. This is a beautiful way to communicate and partner with God.

Another verse I read often as a reminder of God's guiding presence is found in a different psalm. "The Lord says, 'I will guide you along the best pathway for your life. I will advise you and watch over you" (Psalm 32:8 NLT).

First of all, aren't both of these Bible passages full of hope and encouragement? Knowing God's character as teacher, Guide, Savior, and our hope gives us confidence we are in good hands every single day of our lives.

Second, the passage in Psalm 32 reads as a promise. Isn't it wonderful to realize how personal God is? He will guide us down the path that's best for you and me, and He will watch over and advise us as we travel with Him. If we ever question God's motives or intentions, we can simply return to this passage to be reminded of His love and care for us. Don't you appreciate how this verse reminds us He will stay close to us?

God is fully capable of guiding us on every step of this journey. He sees what we cannot. He knows what we do not, and He teaches us what we need to know along the way. He will lead us in learning new ways to stay present with Him by overcoming distractions in our lives. And if a distraction, for whatever reason, is not conquerable, God will give us the capability to stand against it in His strength.

This is about building a vibrant, personal relationship with God.

This isn't about partnering with God to get our way or to achieve something specific. It's not to treat God as a genie in a bottle who lives to grant our every wish. This is about building a vibrant, personal relationship with God. The God of the Bible. The One who created the heavens and the earth in Genesis 1, and the One who formed and made us magnificently as referenced in Psalm 139. The One who gave up His only Son for us as proclaimed in John 3. The One who is making all things new, including you and me as stated in Isaiah 43. The One we can spend eternity with as promised in 1 John 2.

This is the God I'm referencing.

Maybe you're new to all of this "God stuff," or maybe you haven't thought about God in a very long while. Friend, that's okay. There's no shame in that. God is not a God of shame, and He is not mad or disappointed in you. He doesn't exist to punish you. His ways are not our ways, and His thoughts are not our thoughts. We can't begin to comprehend all He is; He's more than our minds can contain. He loves you. He loves me. And He desires His best for us, always. He also desires to spend one-on-one time with each of us.

Building a relationship with God isn't as weird, scary, or difficult as one may think. Just like we grow relationships with people in our lives by spending time with them, we grow our relationship with God by spending time with Him too.

My relationship with God began as a little girl. I guess I always knew God existed, thanks to my parents, but I didn't understand I could have a relationship with Him. To me, God was some unknown figure who lived in heaven and didn't like me very much. At least that was my perception. I was actually scared of Him because I believed I had to say the right prayers, do the right things, go to church, and live perfectly for Him to like me. So a relationship with God seemed unlikely and, certainly, unattainable.

Until one evening when I was with my best friend, Tina, talking to her mom, Barb, on the phone. I was twenty-two years old.

Feeling lost and empty, I was searching and wondering, *is there more to life than this?* I had just gone through a relationship break-up, and I was scheduled to sing in a wedding a week later. *How in the world could I do this?* Life was crashing around me, and there was nothing I could do to hold it together.

Barb shared how there was only One who could fill that space in my heart, how He could take away some of my searching and longing. She shared the truth about Jesus—how He, God's Son, died for me and rose to life again so someday I would rise to new life too. *How could it be? He did that for me?* I desired more! Barb led me through a short prayer, and I asked Jesus to forgive my sins and take control of my life.

Looking back, I don't believe the exact words I prayed mattered as much as the fact my heart was ready. I didn't have the strength to do life on my own anymore, and now I didn't have to. I felt immediate peace.

That was in April of 1991. That evening, Barb said I would experience a joy in my heart that would never leave, and you know what? She was right. That joy is still here today.

Jesus died and rose to new life for me, and He did for you too. I remember Barb's husband, Jim, used to say, "Even if you were the last person on earth, Jesus still would have gone to the cross for you." The truth of that statement still brings me to a place of awe. *Really? He did this for me?*

I share this experience because it's been the foundation of my life. It's the single most important step to my living a life of faith. And it's the basis upon which I can even begin to experience living a truly undistracted life. Friend, I can't guess where you are in your own faith journey, or even if you're on one. I share this out of love. On a simplistic level, it's a bit like possessing an amazing chocolate chip cookie recipe. I desire to share that recipe with others because they deserve to have delicious chocolate chip cookies too. Same goes for my faith. I have been given this amazing gift of faith in Jesus, and I desire to share it with others in my life. Why would I withhold this gift from anyone? I want others to experience the same joy, hope, and grace I've experienced. (It's much better than a delicious chocolate chip cookie, by the way, and in my book, that's hard to beat!)

No matter how you feel about God or faith in Jesus or the message I'm sharing in this chapter, I want you to know God is *for* you. He's not against you. No matter where you are, God meets you. You don't have to clean up, shape up, or make up. He loves you as you are. He will take you by the hand and lead you on the best path for your life like we just read in Psalm 32:8-9. He leads all who follow His Son, Jesus, and He will throughout eternity. He won't give you anything other than His best. What a hope we have!

With us, God may have His hands full, but I believe He'd rather have them full than empty.

I learned that evening in April 1991 that God could love someone like me. Someone who made poor choices as a teenager and tried to live a double life of wild child and good girl. Someone who lived for a good time and wasn't always kind as a young adult. Someone who thought God didn't like me and thought He would punish me if I got too close to Him. It's no wonder I was amazed when I realized God was different than I thought He was. He desired a relationship with me. *How? Why?*

But since that evening, my life has not been all cupcakes and sprinkles—or chocolate chip cookies. All my problems, sins, and heartaches did not magically disappear because I made a decision that evening to live my life with Jesus. That's not what happens when we make that decision. Instead, we're given a hope and a strength we didn't previously possess. Our minds and eyes open to new possibilities we didn't previously know or couldn't see. And when the problems come, we're no longer trudging through them on our own. Rather, we are walking with a helper, a Guide, a promise keeper—the one who won't leave us alone amid our problems.

Let me be clear about something else. My decision that evening hasn't resulted in living a perfect Christian life. Oh, goodness no.

I've made terrible mistakes and sinned more than I care to admit. Yes, even as a Christian. I don't always live the way I know Jesus is leading me to live, and my stubborn streak still likes to be in charge some days.

So why do I share all of this? Because the reality of living for Jesus may be different than what we think it will (or should) look like. This reality includes a security, a hope, and blessing that cannot ever be taken away. No matter what we've done or haven't done, what we do or will do in the future, God loves us. And nothing can change that. With us, God may have His hands full, but I believe He'd rather have them full than empty.

A new beginning starts now. Will you pray with me?

> *God, we need You. We know we cannot overcome these life distractions on our own. We may have tried and attempted to do well for a time, but in our strength, we get weak. We've learned we can't do this by ourselves. Lord, we are asking for Your help. You are the strongest strong One, the wisest wise One. You are the One who knows all, sees all, and is in control of all. You can fight the battles we can't. Jesus, we thank You for dying in our place and rising so we can rise with You some day. Please forgive us for our past mistakes. We put our trust in You and place our hope in You. Lead us by the hand as we take the next steps in removing distractions in our lives. Equip us to live the abundant lives You came to give us. Thank You. In Jesus' name. Amen.*

[PAUSE]

Take a deep breath and pause. Bring your thoughts from wherever they are back to this present moment. Write out what impacted you in this chapter and anything you're noticing.

_____

_____

_____

_____

_____

_____

[PONDER]

Reflect on where you are right now in your faith journey. What's your current relationship with Jesus? Write what comes to your mind.

_____

_____

_____

_____

_____

_____

[PRAY]

Pray the prayer in this chapter, or simply ask Jesus to open your heart to Him and what He has for you. Write it here.

_____

_____

_____

_____

_____

_____

_____

[PRAISE]

Thank and praise God for this new beginning.

_____

_____

_____

_____

_____

_____

_____

7

EMBRACE EACH DAY

What if we begin our day with God?

I love mornings.

I think I always have, for as long as I can remember. Except maybe my first semester in college when I worked in the cafeteria, clocking in by 6 a.m. to help pay for my tuition. Mornings were not my favorite then, cracking eggs and frying donuts, donning a white paper hat with sleep still clouding my eyes.

Other than that season, I do like my mornings. Call me strange, but I get almost giddy when I wake at 5 a.m. and think about the new day ahead of me. I anticipate the possibilities of how God might show up in my life and opportunities I may get to partner with Him. It's as if I wake up to a blank page, and I can't wait to see how we will fill that page together. Yes, I know this 5 a.m. giddy girl is probably in the minority.

I'm guessing you either bound out of bed or you crawl out of it, eventually. Even if you don't work day shift hours, you rise out of bed and begin your day at some point. You may not begin it as early as I do, but you begin it, nonetheless. Regardless of the time, how do you begin your day?

In the past, I've been known to begin my day on the run. This included talking with God on my way to work and counting it as sufficient time with Him. One day a friend mentioned how she spends dedicated time with God every morning. *What does that even mean?* I had no idea. She said she would open her Bible, read it, talk to God, ask for guidance for her day, and pray for those she loved. She blew me away when she said she spends an hour with God some mornings! *What? How do you do that?* Remember, my talking with God happened on my twenty-minute ride to work, and that was the extent of my daily time with Him. I couldn't imagine spending an hour.

It's not that I didn't want to or didn't think it was a good idea, but what on earth would I talk to God about for an hour? My talks with God felt quite one-sided with my long list of requests, needs, and desires. And where would I find that hour? My schedule was already jam-packed. Yet, I knew there had to be more. I knew I was missing out on what my friend was enjoying in her time with God every morning. So that's when I chose to wake up earlier in my day. If I was going to spend "dedicated time with God," it had to be in the early morning hours; otherwise, it likely would get buried in the remainder of the day. *Hello, 5 a.m.*

It felt awkward at first. I didn't know what to say to God or how to spend time with Him. Some days I would open my Bible and just begin reading. Some days I would jot down a few scriptures and thoughts. And some days I would just sit there, listing my requests verbally. Although it felt strange, I kept at it.

The more I did it, the more familiar it became. I began to desire time with Him every morning. It wasn't just a gift to have uninterrupted time alone with God—it became a necessity. That time spent with Him prepared me for the day ahead, and helped me begin the day with His perspective, not my own. It gave me the courage, strength, confidence, joy, and encouragement I needed for the next twenty-four hours.

Over the years, my morning times with God have adapted based on the season I was living. It looked different when the kids were young and at home than it does today. It was different when I was working outside of our home, punching in at the office by 8 a.m. But what I do today, in this current season, is my favorite routine with God so far. It may change a little day by day, depending on my schedule, but mostly, it remains the same.

I guard and keep my morning time with God like an appointment in my planner. It's like meeting a friend for coffee, but instead, I'm meeting God in my home office. During this time, I spend quiet moments with Him, reading my Bible, praying, and journaling. Somewhere along the way, I picked up a habit that has led to journaling my prayers. Each morning, I grab my $2.99 spiral notebook and turn to the next blank page. I write the date on the right-hand side and begin my written prayer with, "Good morning, God!" This is the best way for me to begin time with Him.

Our time together begins even earlier than this appointment. It may sound silly, but each morning when I wake in bed, I desire my first conscious thought to be directed toward my Creator. I usually whisper the same simple greeting, "Good morning, God." Sometimes, silently in my head, I follow with a children's song that contains those words. But with this first awareness of a new day, I offer whatever's on my heart and have a conversation with God before I put my feet to the floor. I absolutely love this moment.

"In the morning, O Eternal One, listen for my voice; in the day's first light, I will offer my prayer to You and watch expectantly *for Your answer*" (Psalm 5:3 Voice).

Each day we need His equipping and guidance if we are going to overcome the distractions that bombard us.

When I'm sitting in my office each morning, I desire this time with God to be unrushed. Some days I spend an hour with Him (yes, can you believe it?), and some days it's less. But I've determined this to be the most important part of my day. I praise and thank Him, pray for any needs, and seek His direction and guidance.

"Let the morning bring me word of your unfailing love, for I have put my trust in you. Show me the way I should go, for to you I entrust my life" (Psalm 143:8).

In the last chapter, we pondered how the path to living undistracted begins with God. This is the natural next step: beginning each day with God. In His strength, in His power, in His grace, and in His will. Each day we need His equipping and guidance if we are going to overcome the distractions that bombard us. We cannot live an undistracted life on our own. With all our might we can try, but we'll not be able to stand alone against these distractions. But in His power and strength we can.

"I can do all this through him who gives me strength" (Philippians 4:13).

When we are weak, He is strong. When we cannot face and overcome these distractions, He can. And through us, He will. When we have Jesus, we have all we need. This is especially true in the battle against distracted living. And it all starts as we begin each day, going to God and seeking His mercies, ones that are new to us every morning.

"The faithful love of the Lord never ends! His mercies never cease. Great is his faithfulness; his mercies begin afresh each morning" (Lamentations 3:22-23 NLT).

God's mercies never run dry. No matter how often we rely on His grace and compassion, more will be waiting for us tomorrow and the day after that. God's new mercies are available to help and address any situation. He loves us too much to let us struggle with these distractions on our own, but He won't force Himself on us. When we start our day with God, asking Him to fill and strengthen us, He'll meet us in every distraction. He'll meet us in every situation. He loves us too much not to.

From personal experience, when I choose to begin my day in a way other than with God, I miss out on so much. I miss the intimacy I enjoy with my Creator. I miss His provision, His infusion of hope and peace, and His blessings. I also miss what He may want to reveal to me, His wisdom, and His direction.

I appreciate what author and coach Chris McClure has to say about this. "If you desire to do your life's greatest work, it needs to start with prayer. God has uniquely designed you to serve Him in your gifts and abilities that He has given you. But if you simply wake up each morning and start being busy, you are likely going to miss out on the blessings and opportunities from God that day."[21]

Amen. This continues to ring loudly: it matters how we begin each day. And it matters that we begin each day with God. It doesn't have to be a big, grand production. It certainly doesn't have to be perfect, or whatever we have conjured up in our minds as "perfect." You and I don't need a prayer closet or separate comfy space to meet with God. We don't have to do anything or be anywhere in particular to spend time with Him. God is already with us. The last words Jesus said to His disciples before ascending to heaven were, "And be sure of this: I am with you always, even to the end of the age" (Matthew 28:20b NLT). This is still true for you and me today.

Simply spending time with God as He directs us and leads us individually is special and intimate. It probably won't look like anyone else's time with God, and that's absolutely okay.

If this is something new to you, or if it's been a while since you began your day with God, it's understandable you may not know what to do. Please don't fret about this. Like I mentioned, time alone with God doesn't have to be perfect or look a particular way. God will show you, and you'll find a rhythm or routine that works for you. Please don't let it intimidate or scare you because God isn't intimidating or scary. I encourage you to have your Bible or Bible app handy and have your phone notifications on silent. We don't need another distraction preventing us from time with God, right? We have plenty of those in this world already.

I suggest starting with a prayer. A simple prayer might sound something like this:

> *Good morning, God! I love You. You are the God who sees me, who knows me, who loves me like no one else. I praise You. You are the One true God, and there is none like You. I thank You for this new day. Lord, I ask You to go before me, to lead, guide, and strengthen me. Please bless me with your wisdom, discernment, and peace. I need You, and I don't want to take one step today without You. Help me to live in each moment You give me, and free me from any distractions that try to snatch my attention away. Lead me to what You have for me in this moment. Teach me in Your ways and Your will. In Jesus' name. Amen.*

God will meet you right where you are. Remember, He is with you already. You could take a step further and open your Bible or Bible app, then ask God to direct you to a passage in the Bible. Take your time reading it. It doesn't have to be a chapter, but simply start with a short passage.

God will meet you right where you are.

Years ago, through Bible Study Fellowship, I learned a specific and simple way to read a passage of Scripture and apply it to my life. I could read the passage, but I rarely understood how to apply it. Sometimes I would read it over and over because I just couldn't understand it. Finding a translation I could understand helped, but this tool aided me immensely. Maybe it'll help you. It involves asking three uncomplicated questions after reading a portion of Scripture.

1. What are the facts? (What's happening in this passage?)

2. What are the lessons? (What can I learn from this passage?)

3. What are the applications? (How can I apply this passage to my life right now?)

Facts. Lessons. Applications. It's straightforward and simple, perfect for my brain. Friend, learning how to study the Bible and apply it to your life doesn't have to be complicated. Sometimes we just need a helpful tool to assist us. I invite you to try this with any Bible verses in this chapter.

God shines through us when we spend time with Him, and we become His light bearers!

If you're a person who likes to journal or desires to begin journaling, you might also try this. Take a simple notebook, write out the passage, then jot your answers from those three questions below it. You'll soon see the Bible in an entirely new and fresh way, and you'll find how much easier it is to apply what you're reading to your life!

This way of reading the Bible completely transformed my time with God and has grown my knowledge of Scripture and my faith. God speaks to me through His Word when I spend this dedicated time with Him. I urge you to give it a try and see for yourself. Incorporating Bible reading into your time with God will help you live in His ways and be undistracted in life. Feel free to add in a devotional or another resource if you'd like, and you'll be equipped for the day.

The day may not go perfectly (because which day ever does?), and it might not go as you plan. But you'll be equipped and strengthened throughout your day because you plugged into your source first. Just like our phones need recharging from a power source every day, so do we. Without plugging into our charging source, our battery runs low and will eventually drain to empty. Let's take as much care plugging ourselves into our "power source" as we do our phones.

Distractions will still come. They will still try to bombard us and attempt to pull us away from what's important in life. They will continue to entice us away from the moment. But we will be less likely to give into those distractions because we aren't operating in our own strength, but in God's. All because we started the day with Him. All because He is our focus and not the distraction.

Now, this isn't to say since we spent time with God in the morning we'll be good to go all day long. Just like our phones, if we use them a lot throughout the day, their batteries will run down quicker than if we don't. So if we're living a full day, experiencing a lot of activities and facing a few distractions, our energy and focus can drain more quickly. And some days we need to recharge our phones before they run empty. Same goes for us. It's good to recharge ourselves by talking with God, seeking His guidance, asking for renewed strength, or thanking Him throughout the day. He replenishes our supply.

The more we spend time with God, the more we'll see how this time not only benefits us, but it helps us to shine God's light in our little corner of the world. God shines through us when we spend time with Him, and we become His light bearers!

> "And you, beloved, *are the light of the world. A city built on a hilltop cannot be hidden. Similarly it would be silly to light a lamp and then hide it under a bowl. When someone lights a lamp, she puts it on a table or a desk or a chair, and the light illumines the entire house.* You are like that illuminating light. *Let your light shine everywhere you go,* that you may illumine creation, *so men and women everywhere may see your good actions,* may see creation at its fullest, may see your devotion to me, *and may turn and praise your Father in heaven* because of it."

> Matthew 5:14-16 Voice

Our time with God not only impacts us, but impacts those around us. We change when we spend time with Him. Our thoughts and our ways become more like His, as well as our attitudes and motivations. We desire more of His will than ours, and we desire to love others in the ways He loves us.

Don't be surprised if those around you notice a difference in you. Don't be alarmed when you suddenly have more patience or understanding. And don't be shocked when the person that used to bug the bejeebies out of you now doesn't seem so offensive.

Spending time with God directly affects everything we do and every part of our lives. No wonder it helps us live undistracted overall.

And no wonder the enemy of our souls wants to keep us away from that time with God in the mornings and throughout the day. No wonder we battle distractions that try to stop us from praying, reading our Bibles, and drawing away to a quiet place with God. Let's face it, if he's not bombarding our thoughts with what's next on our to-do list for the day, he's distracting us in other ways to keep us from plugging into our source. This enemy knows we are weaker when our batteries are facing empty. He knows we're less effective when we're not fully charged. And he knows what will distract us the most.

God is with us, and we must do our part to be strong in Him. The time we spend with God is vital, and I pray you and I do all we can to make it a priority every day. Not only for our benefit but for those around us. We will discuss this more in Chapter 12. This matters, friend, because our lives matter.

Right now matters.

Lord, thank You for reminding us the most important thing we can do to begin our days is to start them with You. Amen.

[PAUSE]

Take a deep breath and pause. Bring your thoughts from wherever they are back to this present moment. Write out what you're noticing.

_____

_____

_____

_____

_____

_____

_____

[PONDER]

How and when do you spend time with God? In what ways might God be prompting you to carve out some time with Him in your schedule, especially in your mornings? How might that look in your life? Write what comes to your mind.

_____

_____

_____

_____

_____

[PRAY]

Seek God and ask Him to help you make time with Him a part of
your day—or help find the best time for you. Ask Him to guide you in
this because He will. Write it out here.

_____

_____

_____

_____

_____

_____

_____

[PRAISE]

Thank and praise God for anything He is revealing to you today regarding spending time with Him and beginning your day with Him.

_____

_____

_____

_____

_____

_____

_____

8

ENJOY PEACEFUL REST

What if we end our day with God?

I wasn't paying attention to what was happening outdoors as I was hastily making dinner. For an instant I lifted my gaze out our north deck doors and saw the most beautiful cotton candy pink-stained clouds. That meant only one thing: the sunset to the west was spectacular. I dropped the paring knife and the carrots, washed my hands, and grabbed my phone. Then I headed to our west windows. I never know what to expect with a sunset. *What will it look like? Will it be filled with colors or just sunbeams?*

I was happy to find this particular sunset was a beauty. No wonder the north sky was filled with pink clouds. I stood there and watched as the sun slowly descended beyond the horizon. Have you ever noticed that the most beautiful part of the sunset happens after the sun has disappeared? It's when the sky fills with some of the most unexpected hues of amber, gold, orange, crimson, and that cotton-candy pink. This one was filled with shades of tangerine with scarlet splashes mixed in. *Click, click, click.* I couldn't quite capture the beauty through my phone's camera, but I certainly tried. Goodness, if I could bottle up a sunset and display it in my home to enjoy all the time, what a gift that would be!

An important part of our day (perhaps the most important) happens after sunset. Not only do the colors of the western sky appear, but it's the time of day where we likely shift to different activities. If you work a different shift than during the day, this may vary for you. But for many of us, our nights consist of rest and sleep. They consist of unwinding from our days and bridge one day to the next. We may not always be awake when the day begins at midnight, but we know whenever we wake for the day, it's already in progress. We can trust no matter what time of day it is, God is always with us and guiding us, including at night.

Goodnight, God. Just like I start the day with, "Good morning, God," I enjoy ending the day with Him, praying, thanking Him, and asking Him for a restful night's sleep. This is the most peaceful and powerful way for me to end the day—ending it with Him. Not only for the current day, but in preparation for the next one.

The distractions we face aren't present just during the daylight hours. Some of the biggest ones knock on the door of our lives at night. Distractions can affect our sleep, and sleep (or lack thereof) affects how we respond to those distractions.

If I was to ask you how much sleep you get on any given night, how would you answer? Years ago an "expert" told me people really only need four hours of sleep each night. I thought I'd give it a try. After attempting four-hour nights, in a matter of days, I had bags the size of suitcases under my eyes. I was falling asleep at my desk. I had no energy and my food cravings were uncontrollable. Maybe some people can get by with four hours of sleep, but not this girl. I need a good seven to eight.

We all know our sleep is important. Sleep stats are just a search away, and through them, we understand why our sleep matters. God wired and designed us to get rest and sleep. We need sleep to regenerate and restore our physical bodies. We need it for our brains to function the way they were designed. We need it for our emotional health and also for our spiritual health. It's important we get enough but not too much.

If we're not getting enough sleep or getting too much, we are more likely to be distracted.

Some of us may remember pulling an all-nighter at some point in our lives. As I think back to the one night in college I tried that, I paid for it days later. My brain was foggy, and I couldn't think straight. My physical body ached, and I remember how dry my eyes felt. My skin looked like I'd aged ten years, and I craved all the foods I normally didn't eat. I remember the effects of no sleep all too well. Maybe you do too.

I also recall the days of raising our children and the 3 a.m. feedings. I remember sleepless nights and napless days. Recently our grandsons had a sleepover at Grandma and Grandpa's, and we had one of those 3 a.m. feedings with our infant grandson. How quickly I forgot about those! Sleepless nights can take a toll. Some seasons in life warrant less sleep, but the one I'm in now isn't one of them. I need my zzz's!

We were designed to sleep; we are well aware of that. Sleep is an important part of our lives, and it's okay to treat it as something we protect and enjoy. It also plays an important part in living undistracted. If we're not getting enough sleep or getting too much, we are more likely to be distracted. In fact, one large study found that people who are sleep-deprived have a much more difficult time overcoming distractions than those who are well-rested.[22]

Research shows fatigue and lack of sleep lowers our brain performance, even with just one sleepless night. It negatively affects our attention, our problem-solving skills, our judgment, and it impairs our ability to quickly switch to other tasks and recall what's stored in our memories. I've also learned we can't "catch up" on our sleep, it doesn't work that way. We can't go on four hours of sleep then "catch up" with a nap during the day.

And did you know multiple well-known catastrophes in history have been linked to sleep deprivation and fatigue? These are a few: the 2005 explosion and fire at the BP Texas City Refinery that killed fifteen and injured over 180, the nuclear releases at Three Mile Island in 1979, Chernobyl and the Space Shuttle Challenger disasters in 1986, and the grounding of the Exxon Valdez oil tanker in 1989.[23]

Think about this: what if your surgeon was fatigued? Your airplane pilot? Your children's bus driver? We trust professionals in our lives to be at their best so they can perform their best, right? Why wouldn't we hold ourselves equally accountable? I don't believe we want to function on low sleep, nor risk potential dangers, depending on our activity. We certainly don't want fatigue to distract us from living the full lives God has for us. You and I don't want to sleepwalk through this life. We don't even want to sleepwalk through one day. Both are just too important.

Constant distraction affects our brains, which affects all we do, including our sleep.

To drive this home further, one study shows one out of three people in the U.S. say they don't get enough sleep, and 83.6 million adults in the U.S. consistently get less than seven hours of sleep in a 24-hour period.[24] Scores of us aren't getting the sleep our bodies require. Why is that? Could one major factor be because we are distracted?

Constant distraction affects our brains, which affects all we do, including our sleep. I'm learning when we experience elevated activity or action, our stress hormones (adrenaline and cortisol) support us. We've all experienced an adrenaline rush, that burst of energy or focus. These hormones also come to our aid when we face distractions throughout our day. But constant distractions can kick them into overdrive where they interfere with dopamine and serotonin, our hormones that allow us to be calm and to relax. This affects our healthy sleep patterns. Constant distractions are affecting more than just our hours while we're awake.

Some nights I have to fight to shut off my brain. On these nights, it wants to keep planning and thinking and wondering like it's done all day. Sleep becomes a battle, and it's one I cannot win on my own. So I pray and ask God to help me fall asleep. Instead of counting sheep, I repeat Jesus' name over and over. I relax my breathing and allow my body to follow. Sleep eventually comes, although it may not be as soon as I would like. Other nights, I wake up somewhere in the middle, and I do the same: pray, breathe, and repeat Jesus' name. Some nights I fall back asleep quickly, but others, I do not.

I understand some of this can be attributed to the season of life I'm living. Some women my age just don't sleep well. Because of this, it's possible we may not always be able to control how we sleep no matter what we do. Our quality and quantity of sleep may depend on our stage of life.

In my case, I wanted to try to get to the bottom of my occasional sleep struggles, so I visited my health care professional. Through a number of tests, I learned my adrenals weren't functioning like they are designed to, and my cortisol levels were elevated. This was directly affecting my ability to sleep. Sometimes we might need to seek a professional to help find the answers we need.

Bedtime used to be when I would strategize and plan for the next day. It used to be the time I dreamed about goals and thought about my future. It also used to be the time I would fret about the past and worry about what's ahead. I learned quickly that bedtime is not the time to be doing any of that. Bedtime is for winding down to rest our minds and our bodies. Thinking, planning, and pondering can be moved to another time of day, one that's not designed for rest.

Are worries or concerns keeping you from sleeping? Do you feel safe and secure when you go to bed at night? Several years ago we purchased an alarm system when our rural county area experienced several break-ins and burglaries. I did not feel safe back then, hence the reason for our purchase. The comfort of knowing our home was protected helped me feel a little more secure. We all know what happens when we hear the slightest noise as we're about to drift off to dreamland. Our minds create scenarios that typically aren't rooted in reality. Before we know it, we've set ourselves into a horror movie scene, and the entire script plays out in our brains from beginning to end. And it never ends well, does it? Do what you can to alleviate any worries or concerns before you head to bed. We don't need those kinds of distractions.

Ultimately, the best thing I can do to feel safe and secure is rest in God's arms as I climb in bed. Some nights I create a picture in my mind of Him holding me so I can rest soundly. The Bible has much to say about resting in God's presence and being safe in His protection.

"In peace I will lie down and sleep, for you alone, Lord, make me dwell in safety" (Psalm 4:8).

"When you lie down, you will not be afraid; when you lie down, your sleep will be sweet" (Proverbs 3:24).

"I lie down *at night* and fall asleep. I awake in the morning—*healthy, strong, vibrant*—because the Eternal supports me" (Psalm 3:5 Voice).

"Since God cares for you, let Him carry all your burdens and worries" (1 Peter 5:7 Voice).

"Come to me, all you who are weary and burdened, and I will give you rest" (Matthew 11:28).

So how can we overcome these nighttime distractions? I made a list of some things I do or have done in the past, and maybe they will help you. Here are ways to prepare for a good night's sleep and alleviate distractions:

- End the day thinking about God, reading Scripture, and thanking Him for the gift of the day.

- Watch the sunset if possible. This helps with our circadian rhythm.

- Journal before falling asleep. This enables us to release anything negative, clear our minds from anything attempting to control our thoughts, and close out the day in a positive way.

- Shut off screens an hour before sleep.

- Drink a soothing beverage an hour before bed. My preference lately is chamomile tea.

- Pray silently or with your spouse. My friend, Deb, suggests asking God for *His* rest. I consistently ask God to help me sleep, but asking Him for *His* rest is a completely different matter. His deep, abiding, lasting rest because as she says, "His rest is much better than ours." Isn't that so true?

- Read something relaxing that's not on a device.

- Prepare your bedroom to be a restful space ahead of time.

- Refrain from watching TV in the bedroom.

- Dim the lights earlier in the evening.

- Adjust the bedroom temperature to be a little cooler, so you don't wake up because you're too warm. (Is this just a mid-life thing?)

- Keep earplugs nearby if you consistently wake from noise in the night.

- Silence your phone or keep it across the room while you're sleeping, if possible.

- Breathe. Take deep breaths in from the diaphragm, counting to four (think of inhaling God's peace). Then exhale slowly, counting to four and releasing any tension.

Find one that works for you and be patient with yourself. Refrain from getting stressed about sleep because that defeats the entire purpose.

Back in high school, I had difficulty falling asleep at night. It was so bad I would lay in bed for hours before sleep arrived. The more I fretted and worried about not falling asleep, the more I couldn't sleep! It was a vicious cycle. One evening, my mom suggested I drink a cup of warm milk before bed. The thought sounded awful, but if Mom (the wisest woman I knew) suggested it, it must work. So in her silver sauce pan with the black-rounded handle, she heated milk on the stovetop until steam began to rise. She poured it into the cup, and I took a sip. It tasted sweeter than cold milk, and it was surprisingly good. I sipped it until it was gone and crawled into bed. I slept like a baby that night.

Now, I can't say for sure if my good sleep was the result of the warm milk or Mom's power of suggestion. But for many nights after, I enjoyed my cup of warm milk before bed—just to be sure. It seemed to cure my insomnia issues.

The Sleep Foundation reports that warm milk might help us with sleep. Studies have shown this to be true, possibly because of tryptophan, the amino acid found in milk which helps in the production of serotonin and melatonin. Serotonin is a neurotransmitter that affects our moods, reasoning, and memory. Melatonin is a hormone released in our bodies at nighttime to help us sleep.[25] It might be worth a try if you're struggling to get some sleep.

Through the years, I've mentioned this warm milk tip in passing conversations and each time I've received the same look of disgust. "Eww, gross!" or "That sounds terrible!" were the responses. Yeah, it sounded gross, but it didn't taste terrible to me.

Again, we must find what works for each of us. We're all different, and what might work for me might not work for you. I suggest praying about it. See what God leads you to do so you get the rest you need.

> *Lord, as I close out this day, would You please give me Your rest tonight? I know I'm safe in Your arms. Amen.*

[PAUSE]

Take a deep breath and pause. Bring your thoughts from wherever they are back to this present moment. Write out what you're noticing.

_____

_____

_____

_____

_____

_____

_____

[PONDER]

Reflect on your sleep and rest. Do you feel you get enough rest, or could this be an area of improvement in your life? Write what comes to your mind.

_____

_____

_____

_____

_____

_____

[PRAY]

Ask God to reveal His best for you regarding your sleep and rest. As you go to bed tonight, ask Him to give you His rest—His perfect, deep, abiding rest. Write it out here.

_____

_____

_____

_____

_____

_____

_____

[PRAISE]

Thank and praise God for any truth He is revealing to you and for any changes He is prompting you to make.

_____

_____

_____

_____

_____

_____

_____

9

TOOLS TO REFOCUS

*What if we could overcome distractions
by using simple tools?*

Living in what some would term "the middle of nowhere," something I enjoy (besides the sunrises and sunsets, of course), is walking on our road. When the Iowa weather permits, I lace up my shoes and take a stroll as often as I can. Not only do I walk for the exercise but also to clear my mind. Our road isn't spectacular. In fact, if you know anything about gravel roads, they get dusty. Very dusty. They are covered with all sizes of gravel pebbles. Our road's smoothness depends on the time of year and how recently the grader has scraped the road. It's not always a fun place to go for a walk, and some might even despise it. On most days I don't mind at all.

One recent morning on my walk, my mind was filled with a long to-do list, and I was questioning if I had time to be out there in the first place. My schedule was packed for the day, and I began to mentally walk through it as I placed one foot in front of the other. As I shuffled along, I realized I wasn't paying attention to my walk. I was distracted by my schedule and mental list, and I wasn't enjoying the walk at all. I either needed to change my attitude or turn around and go home.

I chose the former and decided to make a change. I intentionally began to notice everything around me. Every blade of grass on the side of the road, every size of gravel rock, every smooth place on the road, and every electrical pole I walked by. I lifted my gaze to the sky and noticed every fluffy cloud and how the brightness of the sun made me squint. I paid attention to the coolness of the breeze and the smell from the farm down the road. (I could have done without that, however, since they had just spread manure on the field the day before.)

But I realized something. By noticing the blessings around me, my attitude changed. My schedule hadn't adjusted and my list was still there, but considering the blessings around me helped me appreciate all that was good. Those good things were present all along, but I didn't notice them because I was distracted by what wasn't good. A change in perspective made all the difference.

I wondered what would happen if I applied this same practice to the rest of my day. Would it make a difference in that too? Until the day's end, I fought hard to notice all that was good. It was truly a fight because the distraction of what wasn't good wanted to win in my mind. I battled against my thoughts returning to that staggering list. I struggled against my attention diverting to the pesky fly that kept dive-bombing my head as I worked diligently at my desk. This was war! I questioned if writing the good things down might help, so I took out a sticky note. Every time I noticed a good thing, I jotted it down. Before I knew it, my sticky note was full. There before me, in my own handwriting, were so many good things in my life in that one afternoon alone. How blessed I was to see so much goodness!

This leads us to the first tool to overcome distractions.

TOOL #1: WRITE IT DOWN.

I wondered if noticing the good and writing it down worked to change my perspective, maybe it would work to help me with the everyday distractions I fight against. The next day I kept noticing the good and wrote it down as I went about my day. I also paid attention to what distractions tried to lure me away from my current activity and the moment I was in. There were dozens, and I wrote them down too. Whether it was a thought, my phone, a noise, or my stomach growling, I wrote it down. I didn't know what to expect, but I found writing down these distractions actually helped me ignore them. You wouldn't think that would be the case, would you? But acknowledging the distraction helped me overcome it. Writing it down equipped me to keep my focus on what I was doing and not on the distraction. I couldn't believe it! This was so simple yet worked so well.

I suggest beginning by noticing all that's good in your day. Write them down somewhere—in a notebook, on a sticky note, or log them in your Notes app on your phone. Then do the same when distractions come knocking on your door. Write them down and keep going about your business. You may be surprised to see in black and white the numerous distractions you experience in a day. This little practice may be the perfect tool to help keep you on track. Any new habit may take time to incorporate, but the effort will be worth it.

When I began the act of intentionally noticing the good, it became a habit. Through trial and error, I soon discovered I was creating a toolbox aimed to hinder distractions. This tool, plus the next three, help keep my focus on what matters right now, and they may help you too.

TOOL #2: USE THE FOUR PS.

I began this seemingly trivial exercise a few years ago, and it helps me stay undistracted. It's simple and doesn't take much effort or work. I use it daily, and it has become a beautiful, life-giving habit. I believe it can be life-transforming for you as well.

It's called the Four Ps: Pause, Ponder, Pray, and Praise. We've been using it already at the end of every chapter so you're already familiar with it!

However, there's a little more to it, so let's take a closer look at this tool that can help us live undistracted. With practice, these four steps are quick to walk through. It takes me less than a minute to use now. Let's look at the first step.

[PAUSE]

Wherever you are and whatever you're doing, pause. Stop your activity and lift your eyes. Sometimes the most challenging thing to do in our day is to pause. If it helps, imagine hitting a pause button, and every time you hit it you must halt your activity to be still. Here's your chance to try it out. Pause. Stop. Cease your activity right now.

Okay, did you do it?

That may or may not have been simple for you. Celebrate that small win. Let's move to the second step of this exercise.

[PONDER]

While you're pausing, pay attention to what's happening around you. Ponder what you see. What do you hear? What do you smell? What do you notice? How do you feel?

Go ahead and do this now.

What you notice may seem insignificant or ordinary. Maybe you see a mess on your living room floor from an active day with your children. Maybe you're in the pick-up line at school and your children will be bounding through your vehicle doors at any moment.

Maybe you are sitting at your kitchen table enjoying your first cup of morning coffee. Whatever is happening around you, just take notice.

Pay attention to how you're feeling. Do you feel rushed, stressed, thankful, or blessed? Have you been sitting in one spot for too long and your body is telling you to get up and move around? However you're feeling, or whatever you're seeing, hearing, or smelling, just notice. Ponder. Now move to the third step of this exercise.

[PRAY]

This is a perfect time to talk to God and pray about what you pondered. You might share any feelings you noticed (for example, your frustration with the mess on the floor), any circumstances you realized (such as kids running out of the school building), anything or anyone in your environment you could pray for (like what you noticed while sipping your morning coffee). It doesn't have to be a long, monumental prayer; just have a short conversation with God about anything you pondered. Now to the final step of this exercise.

[PRAISE]

After pausing and pondering and praying about what you noticed, next praise God. Using these three scenarios, let's walk through this together. Praise God for the mess on the living room floor because it reflects where valuable time was spent today. Not only that, but the mess was made by your wonderful children. Praise God for what you pondered in the pick-up line at school. Maybe it was your working vehicle, your kids' school, the white fluffy clouds against the light-blue backdrop sky, or the crimson leaves on an autumn-kissed nearby tree. While you're enjoying your morning coffee at your kitchen table, praise God for what you pondered. Was it the taste of your coffee? Sleep from the prior night? The sun peeking through your window blinds? The warmth of your home?

We have much we can praise God for, right? We can praise Him for the big things, the little things, and everything in between. It all comes from God.

"Every good and perfect gift is from above, coming down from the Father of the heavenly lights, who does not change like shifting shadows" (James 1:17).

"For everything comes from him and exists by his power and is intended for his glory. All glory to him forever! Amen" (Romans 11:36 NLT).

When we stop the rhythm and flow of the day to pause, ponder, pray, and praise, it's as if we document the day. We praise God for the gifts He has given as we notice our everyday life happenings. It's a powerful way to bring ourselves back to the present instead of allowing distractions to overtake us through the day.

This exercise can be done as often as necessary to keep us focused and in the present. We can do this anywhere to recenter our thoughts back to God. The more we do this, the easier and simpler it becomes. It can be a quick habit to incorporate into our daily rhythm.

"Don't shuffle along, eyes to the ground, absorbed with the things right in front of you. Look up, and be alert to what is going on around Christ—that's where the action is. See things from *his* perspective" (Colossians 3:2 MSG).

His perspective makes the difference.

TOOL #3: REFLECT ON TODAY'S DATE.

Another tool I use to help me stay in the moment and live undistracted is one I accidentally began a few years ago. My days felt as if they were running together, and I didn't like it. Time was speeding by too fast, and before I knew it, the day that had just begun was already over! This tool helped me create space in my days. Not only does creating space throughout my day help me live undistracted, but so does creating space between my days. What do I mean by that?

When we stop the rhythm and flow of the day to pause, ponder, pray, and praise, it's as if we document the day.

Do you find your days often run together too? Do they fly by, and the months even faster? Do you, like me, sometimes forget when you first wake up in the morning what day it is? *Is it Sunday or Tuesday?* Maybe it doesn't help that I currently work from home, but sometimes it takes me a few seconds to recall what day it is. *Wait, am I going to church today, or am I working?* Once I figure out the day of the week, it's another task to remember the date. *Is it the 12th or 13th?* I consistently relied on my phone to inform me of the day of the week and the date of the month before incorporating this trick into my day. I call it my "Today's Date" tool.

Here's how it works. Once I wake and remember what day it is, I intentionally recite the date. "Today is Thursday, March 23, 2023." I know, it may seem strange, but stay with me here. I say it again whenever I remember throughout the day—maybe at lunchtime, or while I'm making dinner. "Today is Thursday, March 23, 2023." This cements the day in my brain. It pauses and marks time and causes me to remember *today*. I won't get to the end of the week and think, *where did the week go?* I'll know where it went because I marked the days, all week long.

When we often do the same daily things, in the same routines, the days can easily blend together. We may forget little details we would otherwise notice if it was a memorable day. Marking the day in this manner makes it more significant.

Do we remember what happened in our lives last Tuesday? Can we recall what day we had that important conversation with our spouse? Something as simple as marking the date in our minds can help us recall unimpressive (yet important) moments in our days. Aren't each of our moments important?

Try it out and see how it helps you. Again, this is something that will take some effort to remember to do; after all, it's something new. If this is not an exercise your brain is familiar with, I encourage you to try it once a day. Notice how your days begin to separate themselves and how common, ordinary days will become more memorable in your life. You might also notice time slowing down a bit as you use this tool. Isn't that something we all desire? Another bonus you will gain is the ability to recall important and worthwhile moments you might have otherwise missed because of distractions.

TOOL #4: ENGAGE BRAIN DUMP.

Do you ever experience times when your brain feels so full it might explode? Or feel so distracted your mind doesn't know what to do next? I'm guessing at least once a week I feel this way, and this little trick helps me. I set a timer for ten minutes and take out my notebook. Then I do what I call a "brain dump." I empty everything that's in my brain onto paper. I write down anything and everything I can think of, including those frustrating distractions. I don't worry about grammar or punctuation or even if it makes sense. I just get it all out. Afterward, I usually end with a prayer and ask God to align my thoughts with His. This little exercise doesn't take long, but the benefits are lasting. It clears my mind of distractions, and it helps de-clutter my brain to keep my focus where it needs to be.

Aren't each of our moments important?

These four simple tools may help you live undistracted like they've helped me. I suggest not trying them all at once, but experiment with them, one at a time, and see how they work for you. You'll find one you like best or one that fits you more than the others. Or maybe these will point you to a new idea that's specifically just for you. I pray these suggested tools will help you further your journey in over-coming the distractions in your life.

Lord, guide us as we keep our focus on You and as we in-corporate these tools into our lives. Thank You for helping us live undistracted.

[PAUSE]

Take a deep breath and pause. Bring your thoughts from wherever they are back to this present moment. Write out what impacted you in this chapter and anything you're noticing.

_____

_____

_____

_____

_____

_____

_____

[PONDER]

Reflect on what might help you live undistracted from this chapter. Or if you're not sure, brainstorm ideas of how you can overcome distractions. Write out what comes to your mind.

_____

_____

_____

_____

_____

_____

[PRAY]

Ask God to equip you to apply one tool to help you live undistracted on a daily basis. Continue to seek His help to live in the present moment. Write it out here.

_____

_____

_____

_____

_____

_____

[PRAISE]

Thank and praise God for how He is leading and guiding you today.

_____

_____

_____

_____

_____

_____

_____

10

THINGS ABOVE

What if we keep our focus on what's most important?

In high school, I ran track. I competed in the short races like the 4 x 100 meters, the 4 x 200 meters, and the shuttle hurdle relay. I was terrible at long distance running, and I still am. I'd rather just run as fast as I can for as short as I can and be done. My favorite was the hurdles. Still is, but I'm not sure I could clear them anymore, and I really don't want to hurt myself trying. In my junior year, our relay team of four often performed well at meets, and I still have the medals tucked away to prove it. We quickly found our rhythm and learned how to win races. But our little high school (twenty-seven in my graduating class!) didn't have a running track. We trained around our baseball diamond. Our school was known for baseball, not for track. We did well with what we had.

I learned early that to clear a hurdle without losing speed, what I focused on mattered. It was imperative to keep my sights fixed just above and beyond the hurdle, but never on the hurdle itself. You know as well as I do, whatever we focus on, we follow—in life and in hurdles. I learned this the hard way at one particular meet when, for some reason, a certain hurdle caught my eye. My focus switched to the hurdle, and you can guess what happened, right? Instead of clearing the hurdle, my leading foot hit it dead-on, and I tumbled forward, landing on the cinder block track with the hurdle underneath me. I think I still have scars on both knees to remind me.

What we focus on matters.

What we focus on matters.

Focus is defined as "to direct one's attention or efforts."[26] It also means to "fixate, concentrate, hone in on."[27]

If we think of distractions in life as hurdles, we can follow the same technique I used in high school. To clear the distraction, we don't focus on the distraction. We set our focus above and just beyond it; if we focus on it, we'll hit it every time. Take my word (and my scarred knees) for it. What makes better sense is to set our focus on God and His plans for us instead of the distraction before us.

"Stay focused on what's above, not on earthly things" (Colossians 3:2 Voice).

"What's above" are the things of God, Himself, and His will for us. They contain the good plans He has for our lives. These are considered spiritual or faithful things, such as love, joy, and peace. Some Bible translations refer to these as heavenly things. The earthly things, however, are what seem to capture our attention the most. They are tangible and material items such as our jobs, money, clothing, problems, and yes, distractions. The things above are eternal. They last forever, whereas the earthly things are temporary and will not last.

"So we don't look at the troubles we can see now; rather, we fix our gaze on things that cannot be seen. For the things we see now will soon be gone, but the things we cannot see will last forever" (2 Corinthians 4:18 NLT).

The verse before this reminds us how today's temporary troubles are preparing for us an eternal glory that is greater than anything we can, or will ever, experience here. Our focus matters. We get to choose our focus. We have a say in the matter. We can determine to focus on the earthly things or on the heavenly things. You and I can set our sights on the distractions before us or on God and His plans. Our choice matters because with it comes either blessings or consequences. If we're focused on the earthly things, including distractions, we miss the good God has for us. We miss the priceless moments before us, the intimate experiences of God's blessings, and the special revelations of His love, care, and grace. *How many of these heavenly things have I missed throughout the years because I was focused on the distraction and not on God?*

These heavenly things don't have to be big, life-changing, mountain-moving things. They can be, but they might not be. God sometimes reveals Himself in the small things, similarly to how He did with Elijah in the Bible. Elijah, a mighty prophet of God, was fleeing for his life. After traveling forty days and forty nights, he arrived at Mount Sinai and tucked himself in a cave to safely spend the night. God met Elijah in that cave. This is how God met him:

> *And the word of the Lord came to him: 'What are you doing here, Elijah?'*
>
> *He replied, 'I have been very zealous for the Lord God Almighty. The Israelites have rejected your covenant, torn down your altars, and put your prophets to death with*

the sword. I am the only one left, and now they are trying to kill me too.'

The Lord said, 'Go out and stand on the mountain in the presence of the Lord, for the Lord is about to pass by.'

Then a great and powerful wind tore the mountains apart and shattered the rocks before the Lord, but the Lord was not in the wind. After the wind there was an earthquake, but the Lord was not in the earthquake. After the earthquake came a fire, but the Lord was not in the fire. And after the fire came a gentle whisper. When Elijah heard it, he pulled his cloak over his face and went out and stood at the mouth of the cave.

Then a voice said to him, 'What are you doing here, Elijah?'"

1 Kings 19:9b-13

Sure, God can reveal Himself to us in the windstorms, the earthquakes, and the fires of life, but He also can meet us in a gentle whisper. Sometimes through the whisper is how God gets our attention. If we're distracted by the bigger stuff, we may not hear His voice in the small stuff. Through the sound of a gentle whisper, could God be asking the same to us, "What are you doing here?" Is He calling to us, "What are you doing in the life I've given you? What are you doing to follow me and focus on me? What are you doing here to make a difference for me in this world?" Friend, what *are* we doing here? Take a moment to ponder this question and write down anything God reveals to you.

_____

_____

_____

_____

_____

_____

_____

_____

_____

_____

If we're distracted by the bigger stuff, we may not hear His voice in the small stuff.

After Elijah explained why he was in the cave (likely for his own benefit because God already knew why he was there), God gave him specific instructions and encouraged his heart with hope and promise. He does the same for us, doesn't He? He shows us the next step to take right when we need it, and He encourages our hearts too.

What we focus on matters.

Yes, sometimes the heavenly things are the small things. But we'll miss them if we're distracted. An example is when my young grandson wants my attention to share something he's proud of, but I'm distracted by preparing lunch. Or when I recently observed a husband and wife having dinner at a local restaurant. He couldn't take his eyes off her, yet she was too preoccupied with her phone to notice his loving glances. Or how not long ago my friend realized she was distracted by the suggestions of others regarding her ministry instead of focusing on how God was leading her.

When we focus on the heavenly things, we stay in God's will, function in His strength, and are vessels for His good and His glory. He equips us to live undistracted. This reminds us to place our focus back where it belongs: on God.

"Don't become so well-adjusted to your culture that you fit into it without even thinking. Instead, fix your attention on God. You'll be changed from the inside out" (Romans 12:2a MSG).

How do we do that? How do we fix our attention on God? Just like with anything that's worthwhile, this takes effort. Life on this earth isn't geared toward the heavenly things or the things of God. So fixing our attention on God isn't always the easiest. But with His help, we can do it.

To fix our attention on God, here's a good place to begin: "If any of you lacks wisdom, you should ask God, who gives generously to all without finding fault, and it will be given to you" (James 1:5).

God is the only one who can and will give us wisdom. This isn't just any wisdom, but *His* wisdom. It's wisdom for how to live a steadfast and consistent life, one that honors and glorifies Him. When we operate in God's wisdom, our focus will naturally be on Him and consequently, on the heavenly things.

Following this, we can fix our attention on God by praying and having real and authentic talks with God. We can read our Bibles or Bible apps. We can take part in Bible studies and hang out with others who point us to God. We can get involved at church or attend a small group with others. We can set reminders on our phones to focus on God throughout our days. Living in His wisdom and fixing our attention on God helps us live undistracted. It's the only true way to do so!

Wouldn't it be great if we could peer into the lives of real women who operate in God's wisdom and fix their thoughts on Him? Well, I found some! The Bible contains numerous examples of women who lived undistracted because their focus was on God. Let's take a look.

ESTHER

Esther was a Jew, adopted by and living with her cousin, Mordecai, in Persia. She was chosen to be Queen of Persia by King Xerxes "for such a time as this."[28] Esther's focus was on God and saving her people from annihilation. She remained undistracted as she risked her life to save her people, and she prompted others to fast and pray. Countless lives were spared because of the wisdom God gave her and the bravery she showed in following God's call on her life.

RUTH

Ruth, a Moabite, became a widow after her husband's death. Instead of returning to her people in her homeland, which was the customary thing to do, she chose to live undistracted by staying with her mother-in-law, Naomi, in a foreign land.[29] Naomi's God, the God of the Bible, became Ruth's God by choice. She followed His ways and focused on Him. God rewarded her faithfulness in providing for both Ruth and Naomi. Interestingly, Ruth is one of the five women named in the genealogy of Jesus.

MARY, THE MOTHER OF JESUS

Young Mary, a virgin, was told by the angel Gabriel that she was favored in the Lord's eyes and would conceive and give birth to a son named Jesus. In her young age, she questioned the angel but surrendered her will for God's.[30] Her focus wasn't on herself but on God and His plan for her life and the lives of others. She remained undistracted in living out her calling, despite the circumstances of being unwed and a virgin.

ANNA, THE PROPHETESS

Anna, a widow, devoted her life to serving God in the temple. She stayed focused on God through fasting, prayer, and praise. She lived undistracted to the Lord as she witnessed young Jesus and praised God for the gift of Jesus to the world. She continually talked about the child to everyone who was expectantly awaiting God to rescue and redeem His people.[31] Her words and presence impacted multitudes of people in God's kingdom.

LOIS AND EUNICE

Lois was Timothy's grandmother and Eunice was his mother. It would be easy to miss these two in Scripture because they are only mentioned once.[32] But Timothy's godly upbringing is evident in his life as mentioned in Scripture. It was certainly noticeable by others. This highlights how Lois and Eunice sought God's wisdom and focused on the things of God. They lived undistracted with the purpose of influencing the next generation for Him.

I want to be like Esther, Ruth, Mary, Anna, Lois, and Eunice, don't you? Don't we desire to live the ways they lived, to possess the wisdom of God they possessed, to focus on God the way they focused, and to live undistracted the way they did? Deep down, don't we long to ultimately impact the world beyond ourselves just as they did?

He invites us to live undistracted by keeping our focus on Him.

We can. We don't have to live in biblical times to impact the world around us. We don't need to be a queen, a widow, a virgin, a prophetess, a mother, or a grandmother to affect the lives of others. God calls us just as we are and exactly who we are to make a difference for Him in this world. He invites us to live undistracted by keeping our focus on Him. When we do, we grow personally, and our faith grows exponentially. Others around us are impacted for good, and God receives all the glory. Our focus matters because right now matters.

Lord, help us to fix our minds, our thoughts, and our attention on You and You alone. Help us to live undistracted for our growth, for the good of others, and for Your glory.

[PAUSE]

Take a deep breath and pause. Bring your thoughts from wherever they are back to this present moment. Write out what impacted you in this chapter and anything you're noticing right now.

_____

_____

_____

_____

_____

_____

[PONDER]

Reflect on where your focus has been lately. Have your thoughts been on your circumstances or on God? On your plans or God's plans? What's one thing you can do today to fix your thoughts and attention on God? Write out anything that comes to mind.

_____

_____

_____

_____

_____

[PRAY]

Ask God to show you how you can set your focus on Him daily to live an undistracted life for Him. Write it out here.

_____

_____

_____

_____

_____

_____

_____

[PRAISE]

Thank and praise God for how He is leading and guiding you today.

_____

_____

_____

_____

_____

_____

_____

11

HELPFUL DIVERSIONS

What if distractions could help us?

I met my friend, Tina, for dinner recently, and she gave me something to ponder. She suggested not all distractions are bad. She's a high school teacher and shared how she encourages the students in her class to find a distraction as a healthy outlet for alleviating high school stressors. I remember high school, and I vividly remember the stress. However, I brought some of that stress upon myself as a restless high schooler.

I recall even more vividly my children's high school years, especially since they were more recent. Both of our children experienced stress with classes, friends, grades, and future decisions. We can relate to some of those, right? Imagine the stress high school students experience today. The mounds of homework and studying, pressures of meeting deadlines, excelling in sports, participating in extracurricular activities, the need to earn money by working, more pronounced and defined struggles with mental health issues such as depression and anxiety or disorders brought on by trauma. Not to mention the struggle to fit in, find who they are, to set boundaries, and figure out what to do with their lives (the pressure is real!). In addition, the whole social media scene we never had to deal with where they fight loneliness, isolation and comparison, are excluded and bullied, and have pressure to eat well and maintain a healthy weight. My friend sees more of this than I can even begin to imagine. No wonder students today could use a way to relieve stress.

But can distractions be good? Some say yes and some say no. What do you think? I think they can be. I did an unofficial poll on my Instagram stories recently, asking this same question. Those who responded all said yes. There may be an even better word for "good distractions," and that word is *diversions*. The definition of diversion is "an activity that diverts the mind from tedious or serious concerns; a recreation or pastime."[33] Diversion defines a "good distraction" much better than the word distraction itself.

Am I just splitting hairs here? Well, there's a difference between distractions and diversions, and here is what I've found to be key: it's all in the *why*. When something redirects our focus from whatever we're presently doing, and if we aren't sure if it's something good or not, we can simply ask ourselves *why* we are being distracted in that moment. The answer reveals the underlying issue. *Is this thing pulling me away from my life, or is it making my life better?* Distractions pull us away, and diversions draw us in. Distractions subtract from life, whereas diversions add to life.

Allow me to explain with a story about my daughter, Alissa. After receiving a degree from our local community college, she enrolled in their Emergency Medical Technician (EMT) course. One of the requirements was to do what we call "ride alongs" with local fire departments. On those rides she would receive firsthand experience of what an EMT might face on an emergency call.

She asked a former high school classmate stationed at a local fire department if she could ride along with him. On that ride, she met a young guy who was particularly nice to her. The ride went well and she learned a lot. She went on her merry way and was slated to finish well in the course. But one thing stood in her way. One of the final tests tripped her up, and she wasn't able to pass the course. To do this, she would need to retake the class all over again, which wasn't offered for another year.

Distractions subtract from life, whereas diversions add to life.

This became a huge distraction for her. You can imagine how she felt her life was put on hold and her plans to become a certified EMT stalled. She was disappointed and discouraged. But little did we know, this was only a diversion for a path that would better suit her.

She could have let that distraction of not passing the course deter her. She could have let that distraction control her attitude and future plans. But she didn't. Shortly after, she applied for a job at a local bank and was hired. That job led her down a path of much success and fulfillment within the banking business, having numerous promotions and opportunities for advancement. God blessed her in spite of her own plans not coming together. That distraction became a diversion for God's best.

Oh, and remember that young guy who was so kind to her on that fire department ride along? Well, he eventually asked her out on a date, and a little more than three years later, they married! That young man is now my son-in-law, Morgan. If Alissa wouldn't have taken that ride along, I wonder if they ever would have met. What may seem like a distraction can actually be a diversion! God knows what He's doing, even through unexpected diversions—which can guide us to something better: His best.

Here's one more story about Alissa and another take on diversions. Three years ago, she was pregnant with her first child, and we ordered an inexpensive wall balloon display for her baby shower. As we blew up the balloons the morning of the shower, my daughter had a thought: *I could do this.* She had always wanted to own her own business. She had toyed with different ideas, such as making homemade dog treats or beginning an online shopping site. Never did she think of balloons until the day of her shower. God was planting a seed in her heart that would grow into something she never could have expected or predicted—a beautiful diversion.

For as long as I've known her, she has always thrived from having a creative outlet. Whether that was playing sports in school, playing volleyball in a recreational league, or decorating her home, she has always been creative. It's no wonder God would give her an idea to begin a business with tools in which she could be incredibly creative. Balloons!

Diversions help us cope, positively redirect, and are helpful in releasing stress and anxiety.

In less than six months after she had the *I could do this* thought, she began Bliss Balloons Co. and started creating balloon art to help make this world and those special events in others' lives more fun and beautiful. Bliss Balloons Co. is a perfect, creative diversion from her 9-5 job where she doesn't get to be so creative.

Diversions help us cope, positively redirect, and are helpful in releasing stress and anxiety. For example, take this redirection with my two-year-old grandson. The other day after changing his training diaper, he refused to put on his pants again. Sure, it would have been fine to let him run around home without pants, but the grandma in me thought it was too chilly. So I diverted his attention by discussing the trees outside and how their branches were moving in the wind, almost as if they were dancing. All the while, I slid one foot at a time into his pant legs. Before he realized it, he was wearing pants! I'm not sure he ever noticed.

I also recall how I appreciated the diversions in my life when my mother died years ago. My friends rallied around me (which alone was a great diversion). One in particular had just lost her dad eleven days before I lost my mom. She and I worked together in the same career, and at that time, we were in charge of planning a big event the following month. As we walked through grief and heartache together, we decided to continue planning and hosting the event. We thought it would be a good diversion to help keep our minds on other things than our consuming grief. Sure, we still allowed space for each other to grieve, but we were thankful we had each other and this event to help us cope while focusing on serving others.

Another example is from my friend and mentor Reverend Barbara Furman. She recently wrote and published her autobiography *It Is Well With My Soul: My Story*. In it she shares how two diversions (she refers to them as distractions) helped her in a devastating health diagnosis.

"In the last couple of years, the Lord gave me two enjoyable distractions to keep me from thinking about being sick: genealogy and writing this book. Both became my passions and have helped me take my mind off myself and my pain."[34]

Did you catch how Barb said, "the Lord gave me two enjoyable distractions"? God can use whatever He chooses to accomplish His will in our lives. He is using what she considers distractions to impact the lives of others and to continue making a difference in this world. I personally witnessed how these allowed her not only to cope, but to thrive in life and give her purpose and joy despite her health issues.

Diversions help us with focus. Several studies show how diversions—such as playing games like Tetris—can help with unhealthy food and drug cravings.[35] Have you ever noticed how watching TV or listening to a podcast or music while you're exercising seems to help the workout go smoother and clip along faster? My husband and I were discussing this recently while out on our tandem bicycle. We listen to music through a portable speaker while we're biking, but one evening, we forgot the speaker at home. Without our music, that ride seemed more difficult and lengthier than our other rides. The diversion of music helps us!

Diversions can also relieve stress and anxiety in healthy ways. Maybe you do some of these but have not considered them diversions before:

- Get outdoors

- Listen to an inspiring podcast

- Pray

- Read an uplifting, helpful book

- Watch an encouraging movie or show

- Color, draw, paint

- Help a neighbor

- Write

- Meet a friend for coffee

- Exercise

- Take a nap

- Sit and just "be"

- Laugh

- Connect with loved ones

- Do something that brings you joy

These are all good diversions, don't you think? This is certainly not an exhaustive list, but it gets us thinking about ways we can incorporate healthy diversions into our lives.

Now that we've named them, and now we know diversions can benefit us, which ones will you incorporate into your life? Or if you already use diversions, what's your go-to when you need a break or need to relieve tension or stress? What are some other ways you utilize diversions in your life? When we intentionally use diversions to better ourselves by allowing downtime, relieving stress, or granting permission to interrupt negative thought patterns, habits, or actions, we are choosing them in appropriate and healthy ways.

What are some diversions you can choose to use for good? Write them here.

_____

_____

_____

_____

_____

_____

_____

_____

_____

_____

_____

You already know I walk outdoors when I can, and doing so is one diversion I use when I get overwhelmed or stressed. This helps me focus on something other than bothersome thoughts consuming my mind. It's also mentally, physically, emotionally, and spiritually healthy.

Whether you call them distractions or diversions, it really doesn't matter. But whatever you choose to use for good, entertain them in a deliberate way—not to use them to avoid reality and commitments in life. I also believe diversions can become distractions if we allow them. If I choose the diversion of walking outdoors instead of finishing the task that needs to be finished, that's not using it in a positive way. It would be pulling me away from what I really need to do and would become a distraction. In this instance, walking outdoors would not be the best choice for me. Another example is choosing to clean my desk (a good thing) to avoid writing my next creative piece (the best thing). That's when it becomes a distraction. Asking ourselves why we are choosing this diversion helps us decide if it's the best choice for us at the time. Is it a distraction or a diversion? Is it harmful or helpful, depleting or hopeful, detrimental or healthy?

Bottom line: if it's not bettering our lives, we may need to reconsider how much time we allow ourselves to entertain it.

It's wise to ask these questions regarding anything we allow in our lives. This could be technology, phones, social media, TV, overworking, or anything else. Bottom line: if it's not bettering our lives, we may need to reconsider how much time we allow ourselves to entertain it.

So yes, distractions (or rather, diversions) in our lives can be good. Let's just make sure we are using them in positive ways.

Lord, open our eyes to see what diversions helpful and positive and which distractions are not. Please give us Your wisdom and discernment to know the difference.

[PAUSE]

Take a deep breath and pause. Bring your thoughts from wherever they are back to this present moment. Write what impacted you in this chapter and anything you're noticing right now.

_____

_____

_____

_____

_____

_____

[PONDER]

Reflect on any diversions you go to when you need to pause, redirect, cope, or relieve stress. Are they helpful? If you don't use any at this point, what might you consider from the list of ideas in this chapter? Write out what you're thinking.

_____

_____

_____

_____

_____

_____

_____

[PRAY]

Ask God to show you how He may be using diversions for good in your life and how you can perceive them with hope and promise. Write it out here.

_____

_____

_____

_____

_____

_____

[PRAISE]

Thank and praise God for how He is leading you to incorporate healthy diversions into your life.

_____

_____

_____

_____

_____

_____

12

NOT ALWAYS ABOUT US

*What if we desire to bless others
by living undistracted?*

R ight now matters because living in the moment allows us to be spontaneous. It frees us to be used by God in the ways He desires, which may look different than what we expect. Living in the moment enables us to see others through God's eyes and not through our own tinted lenses. It gives us opportunities to be blessings in this world and to be compassionate toward other people. Living in the moment helps us be the hands and feet of Jesus every single day. Embracing this kind of life allows an openness to notice the needs of others, the silent pleas for help, and the missed signals of someone who needs a friend.

But if we're living distracted, we don't see it. We miss these kinds of occasions to bless and help. We don't notice the needs of others because our eyes are blinded by what's distracting us. We aren't open to God's use when we're preoccupied with our own problems. We are unable to be attentive to the subtle signals of others when we're distracted. We miss the special opportunities God has in front of us.

Living in the right now isn't always just about us. We may think it is, and there's nothing necessarily wrong with that. Living undistracted, however, takes on an entirely different meaning when we are motivated to love, serve, and bless others. It's not always for our own benefit, but maybe the gift of living undistracted is exemplified when it benefits others more than ourselves.

Living in the right now isn't always just about us.

What do I mean? When I served in a local mission for about five years of my life, people who were homeless and anyone in need entered to receive assistance and hope. I learned early that if I was not in tune with God's guiding presence, and if I did not release the distractions in my mind or in front of me, then I could not serve well. The people needed groceries, a hot meal, prayer, or someone to talk to, but if distractions clouded my vision or my thoughts, I couldn't be fully present for the very people God placed in front of me to serve.

I took each encounter with the patrons of this mission as an encounter from God. I believed He placed each one in my path for a reason, and I desired to serve that person as if I were serving the Lord.

"Work willingly at whatever you do, as though you were working for the Lord rather than for people" (Colossians 3:23 NLT).

I could not be distracted. I had to choose to be present in the moment. Some days that was easier said than done. Every day I needed to surrender the distractions in my own personal life and the things that weighed me down to God so I could be fully present for the person in front of me. Some days that meant listening to someone's life story for the 12,000th time or helping a family in the food pantry with groceries for their home. Other days it was sitting with someone to encourage him during our noon meal, or praying with a hurting soul who needed a reminder God had not given up on her.

The truth is this: the people in our lives need us to be present. This applies to those in our home, at our work, or those in our social circles; they desire our full attention. It's the same for the people we serve, the person on the other end of the phone, or the one receiving our email. They need us to be fully engaged, not half-listening or half-paying attention. They need us to be in communion and communication with God. If we aren't fully engaged, then the people we do life with only receive half of us, if that. And when that happens, we short-change them. That's when we (unintentionally) treat them as if they don't matter. We don't give them our best. They know it, and so do we.

What if God wasn't fully present when we talk to Him? What if He was too busy or distracted by all He had to do? What if He didn't pay attention to us and wasn't really listening to what we had to say? How would that make us feel? Have you ever had this happen with another? You were having a conversation with someone and she became distracted, not fully present in the conversation? Maybe a notification from her phone or an interruption of some sort took her attention away. Or you were in the middle of a sentence and the person you were talking to took her focus off of you and put it on someone else.

This has happened to me numerous times. One instance I remember vividly. My daughter and I were meeting her fourth-grade homeroom teacher during a meet and greet night a few days before the school year began. Our daughter was given the opportunity to locate her homeroom, bring her school supplies, and find her locker. We introduced ourselves to her teacher and were enjoying a wonderful conversation. I was mid-sentence when the teacher's eyes wandered away and fixated on another parent and child in the classroom doorway. Her body followed, and I never got to finish that sentence.

It's interesting how God uses situations like that for our own good. The experience left me feeling unimportant, unseen, and looked over. That evening, I desired to never cause anyone else to feel that way. Yet I did a similar thing just last weekend. Sitting across from an acquaintance, talking with her, I heard a familiar voice to my left. I looked up and there was the husband of my best friend! *What? What is he doing here? If he's here, then my best friend must be here!* I got up and gave him a hug as I was mid-sentence with the acquaintance across the table. *Ugh!* I immediately became aware of what I did. Instantly, the fourth-grade meet and greet resurfaced in my memory. I sat back down and apologized to her. I felt terrible and told her so. *Jesus, help me.*

Right now matters. How important it is to live undistracted in the moment and not be enticed away by other things or thoughts! Others deserve our undivided attention. Right now matters because the people God places in front of us matter.

Jesus modeled staying present well. The Bible is full of these examples, and we can learn from them. He wasn't distracted when He fed the five thousand. He wasn't distracted as He let the little children come to Him. He stayed in the moment when He reclined with His disciples at the Last Supper. He wasn't distracted as He noticed the blind, the lame, the demon-possessed, and even Zacchaeus in a sycamore tree. And He certainly wasn't distracted as He carried His cross to Calvary. Jesus was filled with purpose and passion and saw the heart of each individual. Take for example, the woman who touched His cloak and was healed after bleeding for twelve years. He stopped in the bustling crowd to address her and tell her she was healed. We see this same intentionality with the man lowered through the roof of the house where Jesus was preaching. Jesus paused and saw the man in need and healed him. In every single account we read of Jesus, we never see Him distracted. Instead, we always see Him living in the moment, always present, doing the work of His Father.

I want to be more like Jesus. How about you? I want to stay in the moment and be present with the people He sends my way. I want to embrace every daily moment He gives me and be able to lay my head on my pillow each night knowing I lived undistracted that day. Maybe you, too, desire to notice like Jesus noticed, to be present like Jesus was present, to love like Jesus loved, and to live undistracted like Jesus did.

You and I aren't Jesus, but if we love and follow Him and believe He is our Savior, the same power present with Him is present in us. Living undistracted isn't easy, but with Him as our example, and with the power of the Holy Spirit residing in us, we can do this. Yes, it will take work, and it will take effort. Some days we'll likely feel like giving up and giving in. But the people in our lives deserve our undistract-ed, undivided attention. They deserve our intentional presence. And God deserves our uninterrupted presence as well.

So let's practice being present and staying in the moment. Let's not let our thoughts or emotions wander to the past, the future, or what's on our to-do lists. May we not only do this for us, but also for the sake of others. As we practice, we will get better, to the point it's no longer a practice, but has become a way of life. Right now matters because living like Jesus for the benefit of others matters.

Living in the moment is not always about us. It's more about others and connecting with those around us. Living undistracted greatly impacts our own lives, but it largely influences the lives of others too. And that, my friend, is an amazing and priceless gift!

I wrote this poem a number of years ago. I can't remember when or why, and I don't think I've written another poem since. Maybe God had it in mind for this very chapter all those years ago. It seems perfect and timely for this chapter and for us today. Turn to the back of this book to access the free printable in the Appendix.

Lord, Help Me Be a Blessing Today

Lord, help me be a blessing today.

Help me to lessen the load of others.

Equip me to encourage and cue me to show compassion.

Where I can, help me walk alongside those who need a friend with a listening ear and a helping hand.

Help me to not add to the burden of any person in any way.

Allow me to voice words of sympathy, sorrow, and caring.

Help me also speak blessings, compliments, and congratulations where I'm able.

Give me a heart to comfort and not compare, to serve without strife.

Lord, open my eyes to the ones who feel invisible.

Allow me to see those who aren't seen.

May I notice those who feel unnoticed.

*Lead me to love without conditions,
believe the best in others,
and shine Your light to everyone I meet.*

I pray others see Jesus in me today.

In Jesus' name. Amen.

[PAUSE]

Take a deep breath and pause. Bring your thoughts from wherever they are back to this present moment. Write out what impacted you in this chapter and anything you're noticing right now.

_____

_____

_____

_____

_____

_____

[PONDER]

Reflect on how distractions have pulled you away from giving your best to others in the past and commit to staying present in the moment for their benefit. Write what comes to your mind.

_____

_____

_____

_____

_____

_____

[PRAY]

Ask God to prompt you whenever you're with others and are not fully present in the moment. Continue to pray for His help in living undistracted. Write it out here.

_____

_____

_____

_____

_____

_____

_____

[PRAISE]

Thank and praise God for how He is expanding your knowledge and understanding regarding living distracted.

_____

_____

_____

_____

_____

_____

_____

13

OUR TROWEL AND SWORD

What if we pray as we work?

O ur son, Zach, now an adult, made a side comment a couple years ago that surprised me. I can't remember exactly what we were discussing at the time, but he said every morning he leaves his home fifteen minutes early for work to sit in his car to read his devotional book and pray. *What? Really? What twenty-four-year-old guy does that?* Well, this one. My son understood the importance of prayer and spending time with God before stepping through the doors at work. I recently asked him about this practice, and he said he still does this daily. Prayer matters.

Prayer matters to God and to us. Prayer is simply talking with God. It's the primary way we connect and communicate with Him. I've heard it described as the communication of the human soul with the Creator of that soul. Prayer is a gift, and we're invited to talk with God throughout our day. He invites us to come to Him with all of our needs, concerns, and cares. We can talk with Him about anything: not just the bless-me-today-Lord kind of prayers, but more of the I-can't-do-this-day-without-You-Lord kind of prayers. We can pray not only the keep-me-safe-today prayers, but also the I-can't-overcome-these-distractions-on-my-own prayers.

In the Bible, a man named Nehemiah understood this probably more than I ever will. To give you a little background, Nehemiah, a cupbearer of the king of Persia, was motivated to travel to Jerusalem to rebuild its wall after receiving a report from his brother it had been torn down and the gates burned. After praying and receiving both the king and God's blessing to go, Nehemiah arrived in Jerusalem and re-cruited help to begin working on the wall. The book of Nehemiah re-cords numerous obstacles and occasions when Nehemiah turned to God in prayer for His strength and help. Nehemiah knew he couldn't possibly rebuild the wall without God's leading and assistance, but he fully believed "the God of heaven will give us success."[36]

Facing much distraction, internally from the workers and exter-nally from their enemies while receiving reports of planned enemies' attacks, Nehemiah continued to turn to God. The Jews worked on the wall from sunrise to sunset, fully prepared for ominous attacks from their enemies. Simultaneously, they built the wall and readied themselves to fight. They worked with one hand and carried a sword in the other. Long ago, I heard it described as they held two tools rebuilding the wall. One hand held a trowel (a small-handled shovel), and one hand held a sword. We also have two similar tools: a trow-el of sorts in one hand to partner with God in living undistracted, and we have what Paul in Ephesians 6 describes as the sword of the Spirit, the word of God, in the other hand.

"Take the helmet of salvation and the sword of the Spirit, which is the word of God" (Ephesians 6:17).

This word of God in Ephesians 6:17 in the original language is *rhe-ma*, meaning "spoken word." Another word is used in Scripture for the Word of God, such as in John 1:1, and that is *logos*, meaning the inspired written Word of God and Jesus Christ. In Ephesians, Paul is stating the sword of the Spirit means not just the written Word of

God but speaking the word of God in however He reveals it to us. Power is found in God's word when we speak it directly into the situations we face—a power our words do not have. One way we speak the word of God is through prayer. Just like my son does, and just like Nehemiah did.

God helped Nehemiah and the Jews succeed in rebuilding the wall—in just fifty-two days! They succeeded beyond that when their enemies shrunk back in fright and humiliation for what God had done through Nehemiah and the people. God helps us as we carry out His will for our lives, simultaneously in prayer.

As we've already learned, we cannot fight our spiritual enemy or fight life's distractions on our own. Nehemiah knew they couldn't fight their enemies and finish the wall on their own either. We need God's presence and power, just like Nehemiah did. We need to carry the sword of the Spirit with us as we work. But how do we do that? We speak the word of God.

We work, and we pray. We pray as we work.

What if we've not done that before or what if those words, "speak the word of God" sound bigger than what we think we're capable of doing? They may even sound a little scary or unnerving. *How in the world do we do that, and why would we want to? Isn't God the only One who speaks His word?* Because God's power and authority are present in His words, and when we speak them, we are claiming His authority and power in our lives. God gives His words to us so we can live in them and through them.

Here is one way how. Below are ten Bible verses we can read and speak to help us overcome distractions in our lives. I've also included a prayer below each one to pray in this battle against distractions. This is how we carry a trowel and a sword with us daily. We work, and we pray. We pray as we work.

[1]

"Be very careful, then, how you live—not as unwise but as wise, making the most of every opportunity, because the days are evil" (Ephesians 5:15-16).

PRAY THESE VERSES

Lord, distractions have been keeping me from using the time You've given me wisely. I have not been careful in how I've been living, but I've allowed these distractions to sidetrack my focus. Please forgive me and help me make the most of every moment today, to overcome evil, and to live out the calling You have for me. I desire to glorify You. Amen.

---

[2]

"I am saying this for your benefit, not to place restrictions on you. I want you to do whatever will help you serve the Lord best, with as few distractions as possible" (1 Corinthians 7:35 NLT).

PRAY THIS VERSE

Lord, my heart's desire is to love and serve You, yet many distractions entice me away from doing that. Please guide my thoughts today to keep them fixed on You and how You want me to serve You and others. Help me stay focused on You and Your plans for my life. You know what's best for me, so I trust You and Your will. Amen.

---

[3]

"So do not worry, saying, 'What shall we eat?' or 'What shall we drink?' or 'What shall we wear?' For the pagans run after all these things, and your heavenly Father knows that you need them. But seek first his kingdom and his righteousness, and all these things will be given to you as well" (Matthew 6:31-33).

PRAY THESE VERSES

Lord, the things of this world distract me so often and prevent me from seeking You. I'm sorry I've let those distractions win in the past, but today I ask You to release my grip on the worldly things and to cling to You instead. I know when I seek You, You will give me all I need, even the power to overcome distractions in my life. Thank You. Amen.

---

[4]

"Very early in the morning, while it was still dark, Jesus got up, left the house and went off to a solitary place, where he prayed" (Mark 1:35).

PRAY THIS VERSE

Lord, I can't live any part of this day in my own strength. The world tells me I can, but I've proven I can't. I need You. Jesus, as You often withdrew to an isolated place to pray and to spend time with Your Father, please help me do that as well. I desire to hear Your voice right away each morning and to receive Your strength to live an undistracted life to glorify You. Amen.

---

[5]

"Let your eyes look straight ahead; fix your gaze directly before you. Give careful thought to the paths for your feet and be steadfast in all your ways. Do not turn to the right or the left; keep your foot from evil" (Proverbs 4:25-27).

PRAY THESE VERSES

Lord, I know where I focus I will follow. I desire to follow You, not what distracts me to follow lesser things. Please help me to keep my eyes fixed on You today. Lead my every step so I don't get sidetracked and help me to stay on Your path. Keep me away from what's evil, so I can fully enjoy Your presence. Thank You. Amen.

---

[6]

"No temptation has overtaken you except what is common to mankind. And God is faithful; he will not let you be tempted beyond what you can bear. But when you are tempted, he will also provide a way out so that you can endure it" (1 Corinthians 10:13).

PRAY THIS VERSE

Lord, this world is full of temptations, yet Your Word says You will not allow me to be tempted beyond what I can handle. You will always show me a way out or a way I can endure the temptation. Please help me to stand against distracting temptations that come my way. Equip me in Your wisdom and strength, and help me to encourage others in the temptations they face. Amen.

---

[7]

"So I say, let the Holy Spirit guide your lives. Then you won't be doing what your sinful nature craves. The sinful nature wants to do evil, which is just the opposite of what the Spirit wants. And the Spirit gives us desires that are the opposite of what the sinful nature desires. These two forces are constantly fighting each other, so you are not free to carry out your good intentions" (Galatians 5:16-17 NLT).

PRAY THESE VERSES

Lord, You know my heart. You know my intentions. Yet as Your Word states, if I don't let the Holy Spirit guide my life, I will always follow my sinful nature. Please help me to live according to the Holy Spirit today, to rise above the distractions of my sinful nature, and to trust You to help me carry out my good intentions. Amen.

---

[8]

"If any of you lacks wisdom, you should ask God, who gives generously to all without finding fault, and it will be given to you" (James 1:5).

PRAY THIS VERSE

Lord, Your wisdom is far above any earthly wisdom, including my own. Your Word says I can ask You for Your wisdom, so I come to You today in prayer, humbly asking for this amazing gift. I desire to use it to be alert and aware of when distractions try to rob me of what You have for me. I desire to live a life that honors You. In Your wisdom, equip me to do that today. Amen.

---

[9]

"Think about the things of heaven, not the things of earth" (Colossians 3:2 NLT).

PRAY THIS VERSE

Lord, life on earth is full of so many distractions. People and places, material and temporary things, needs and wants, circumstances and situations—they all entice me away from the eternal things that You've called me to focus on. Please help me keep a heavenly focus today, not an earthly one. Help me to remember what's ultimately and eternally important. Amen.

---

[10]

"Don't copy the behavior and customs of this world, but let God transform you into a new person by changing the way you think. Then you will learn to know God's will for you, which is good and pleasing and perfect" (Romans 12:2 NLT).

PRAY THIS VERSE

Lord, I have copied the ways of this world for far too long. Please forgive me and align my thoughts with Yours today. Because I know much of what I do and the distractions I allow in my life begin in my head, I ask You to transform me through my thoughts into the person You desire me to be. May I learn Your will for my life as You do. Thank You. Amen.

Speak these words of life out loud. Recite the prayers out loud. Speak them directly into your current circumstances and situations. When you and I do this, we invite God, His presence and power, into the fight against distractions. We are no longer fending for ourselves! Are you as glad as I am that we're not on our own in this? A trowel and sword. One in each hand. Both are necessary in living an abundant life on this earth. We work and we pray and we overcome the distractions in our lives to finally live an undistracted life. Turn to the Appendix to access free printable cards containing these Scriptures and prayers.

Lord, thank You for Your word—both Your written Word and spoken word—and for how You call us to use this sword of the Spirit. Help us to do this daily. Amen.

[PAUSE]

Take a deep breath and pause. Bring your thoughts from wherever they are back to this present moment. Write out what impacted you in this chapter and anything you're noticing right now.

_____

_____

_____

_____

_____

_____

[PONDER]

Reflect on how Nehemiah and others rebuilding the wall carried a trowel in one hand and a sword in the other. How does this (working and praying simultaneously) apply in your current circumstances regarding distractions in life? Write what comes to your mind.

_____

_____

_____

_____

_____

_____

[PRAY]

Ask God to equip you through His Word with the above Scriptures and prayers to overcome distractions and to live the abundant life Jesus came to give you. Write it out here.

_____

_____

_____

_____

_____

_____

[PRAISE]

Thank and praise God for how He is present and powerful in your life and doesn't leave you to fend for yourself regarding overcoming life's distractions.

_____

_____

_____

_____

_____

_____

14

RIGHT-NOW WOMEN

What if we live as Right-Now Women?

Well, here we are. We made it to the final pages. Goodness, we've journeyed through a great deal together. You and I covered much ground and are now empowered to live undistracted lives! I have a term for women who are brave enough to venture into this new way of living. We who are ready to do what it takes to be present in the current moment and experience all God has for us right now, and who are motivated to live undistracted lives for our good and the good of others. We who are inspired and determined to trust God every step in this living undistracted journey, and who are willing to extend ourselves beyond what we know to grow into the women God created us to be. We are what I call, Right-Now Women.

Who is a Right-Now Woman? She is you. She is me. She is not flawless or faultless, nor does she have the living undistracted way of life perfected. She understands living in this culture of distraction as a Right-Now Woman can be a challenge. She's willing to trust God as He leads and guides her in this new way of living. Trusting His ways and relying on His strength and not her own, she is eager to embrace the life she's given right now. She understands right now matters.

How does a Right-Now Woman live? How does she function in everyday life? We can glean from an example of a Right-Now Woman in the book of Proverbs. We don't know this woman's name, and we won't attempt to compete or contend with her. Peering into her life recorded in Scripture, however, we can see how she is a Right-Now Woman. Maybe we can learn and apply something from her example in our own lives. She's known as the Proverbs 31 Woman.

> *Who can find a truly excellent woman?* One who is superior in all that she is and all that she does? *Her worth far exceeds that of rubies* and expensive jewelry.

> She inspires trust, and *her husband's heart is safe with her, and* because of her, *he has every good thing.*

> *Every day of her life she does what is best for him, never anything harmful or hurtful.*

> *Delight attends her work and guides her fingers as she selects* the finest *wool and flax* for spinning.

> *She moves through the market like merchant ships that dock here and there in distant ports, finally arriving home with food she's carried from afar.*

> *She rises* from bed early, *in the still of night,* carefully *preparing food for her family and providing a portion to her servants.*

> She has a plan. *She considers some land and buys it; then with her earnings, she plants a vineyard.*

> *She wraps herself in strength,* carries herself with confidence, and works hard, *strengthening her arms* for the task at hand.

She tastes success and knows it is good, and under lamplight she works deep into the night.

Her hands skillfully place the unspun flax and wool *on the distaff, and her fingers twist the spindle* until thread forms.

She reaches out to the poor and extends mercy to those in need.

She is not worried about the cold or snow for her family, for she has clothed them all in warm, *crimson* coats.

She makes her own bed linens and clothes herself in purple and fine cloth.

Everyone recognizes her husband in the public square, and no one fails to respect him *as he takes his place of leadership in the community.*

She makes linen garments and sells them in the market, *and she supplies belts for tradesmen* to carry across the sea.

Clothed in strength and dignity, with nothing to fear, *she smiles* when she thinks *about the future.*

She conducts her conversations with wisdom, and the teaching of kindness is ever her concern.

She directs the activities of her household, and never does she indulge in laziness.

Her children rise up and bless her. Her husband, too, joins in the praise, saying:

'There are some—indeed *many—women who do well* in every way, *but of all of them only you are truly excellent.'*

Charm can *be deceptive and* physical *beauty will not last, but a woman who reveres the Eternal should be praised* above all others.

Celebrate all she has achieved. Let all her accomplishments publicly praise her.

Proverbs 31:10-31 (Voice)

See what I mean? Her life is proof she is a Right-Now Woman—a woman who lives undistracted and embraces every moment. She lives purposefully and intentionally and partners with God to serve Him and those around her. She honors her husband, delights in her work, and isn't afraid of getting her hands dirty. She plans her work and works her plan and makes the most of every day. She is focused. She cares for her household and for the needy. She reveres God and honors Him with her life, all while making the most of what He's given her. I believe the ultimate truth to living as a Right-Now Woman is found at the end of that Scripture: "Charm *can* be deceptive and *physical* beauty will not last, but a woman who reveres the Eternal should be praised *above all others*" (Proverbs 31:30 Voice).

As from this woman's example, living as a Right-Now Woman doesn't have anything to do with residing in a clean and beautiful house or raising perfectly mannered children. It's not about our marital or social status. It's not even about striving the hardest or having tons of money or acquiring nice things. This is about rising up in our current culture as women who seek God in all we do and for all we need. We trust Him with our very lives and allow Him to mature us in this way of living undistracted, daily.

Lysa TerKeurst, founder of Proverbs 31 Ministries, has this to say about this woman in Proverbs:

"But what if I told you that the heart behind Proverbs 31:10-31 is one of celebration, not condemnation?

The first thing I want us to take note of is that this isn't just a chapter about a wife of noble character, despite how your Bible titles verses 10-31. It's a chapter about a woman of valor. A courageous woman. A woman of strength and dignity.

In Jewish culture, these verses are read out loud on the Sabbath as a celebration over the women. This is in no way condemning what they aren't but celebrating how they are, in their own unique expressions, living out the virtues detailed in this chapter. These aren't words meant to tell a woman she is supposed to be more. They are a celebration of who she is."[37]

For years, I measured myself against the Proverbs 31 Woman. I tried to do "all the things" to be more like her. However, God isn't asking us to do more or be more. He simply wants us to follow Him. As we look at this woman in Proverbs 31, we can celebrate who we are as Right-Now Women. We are women of valor, courage, strength, and dignity. We are not this way from our own efforts, because we know we can't possess these characteristics by ourselves. We possess these qualities because of the God we love and serve, the presence of Jesus in our lives, and the power of the Holy Spirit. This is how and why we are Right-Now Women. And because of this, as this Scripture refers, you and I have every reason to smile and have hope when we think about the future.

We are women of valor, courage, strength, and dignity.

What does that future look like? We don't fully know, but we understand God will lead us there. As we take bold steps to apply what we've learned in the previous pages, we can trust our futures will be different and more fulfilling than our pasts. Living undistracted provides us more joy, more priceless moments, and more of God's amazing peace. We will truly be able to live the abundant lives Jesus came to give us. Of course, we don't expect life in the future to be all sunshine and roses. But no matter what comes our way, God will not leave us; rather, He will equip us to live the undistracted lives He's calling us to.

We have a choice to make each day. Will we choose to live as Right-Now Women, or will we continue to live distracted and potentially miss blessings the Lord has for us? Because you've gotten this far in your reading, I believe you want to join me in living as a Right-Now Woman. The following statements will help us stay on track. The business world may refer to them as "power statements." Power statements are assertions or summaries of who you are—your values, strengths, needs, and preferences all wrapped up into a strong, meaningful statement. Others might call them affirmations. An affirmation declares the truth of something. So I call these our "Right-Now Women Affirmations." Twenty-two affirmations are below and declare the truth of who we are in this new way of living. Put a check mark next to the ones that mean the most to you.

▢ Right-Now Women live undistracted for God and His glory.

▢ Right-Now Women live undistracted for the good of others.

▢ Right-Now Women live undistracted for our own growth.

▢ Right-Now Women live undistracted for our marriages.

▢ Right-Now Women live undistracted for the next generation.

▢ Right-Now Women live undistracted to notice the best in others.

▢ Right-Now Women live undistracted because we believe our breakthroughs are coming.

▢ Right-Now Women live undistracted so we see the Lord at work in our lives.

▢ Right-Now Women live undistracted so we believe the best of ourselves.

▢ Right-Now Women live undistracted so we can create beautiful memories with others.

▢ Right-Now Women live undistracted to make a difference in this world.

▢ Right-Now Women live undistracted to live more efficient and effective lives.

▢ Right-Now Women live undistracted so we can serve the Lord with passion and purpose.

▢ Right-Now Women live undistracted so we can serve others attentively.

▢ Right-Now Women live undistracted to be examples for other women.

▫ Right-Now Women live undistracted to be able to speak the truth in love.

▫ Right-Now Women live undistracted so we can forgive ourselves and others.

▫ Right-Now Women live undistracted so we can follow God's plans for our lives.

▫ Right-Now Women live undistracted to be our healthiest selves.

▫ Right-Now Women live undistracted to enjoy the lives we've been given.

▫ Right-Now Women live undistracted because we realize we get one chance to live this moment, this day.

▫ Right-Now Women live undistracted because right now matters.

You and I aren't the same women we were when we began reading this book. We are altered. We are changed. God has opened our eyes to our distracted reality. We've faced it and have decided to make a change and live differently. We know the distractions will still come, but we're equipped to see them, face them, and overcome them with the tools we've been given. With God's help, distractions will not run and rule our lives any longer.

You and I are now empowered to embrace a new lifestyle as Right-Now Women.

As Right-Now Women, we understand when we live undistracted, we live differently. We have more patience, empathy, joy, and hope than we do when we're bogged down by distractions.

We believe when we live undistracted, we are able to seek God and His will for our lives. We trust Him as He leads us and guides us to that will. Living in this way clears out the clutter so we can walk closer with our Lord.

We have learned that when we live undistracted, we are less enticed to focus on the earthly things, and instead, keep our gaze on the heavenly things.

We affirm when we live undistracted, we are better able to care for ourselves, for others, and for the world around us because we live in the moment and stay present.

We are excited to embrace the truth that living undistracted means we are open to making a difference in the lives of other people. We see their needs, we hear their concerns, and we feel the weight they've been carrying. Living in this manner opens opportunities to show God's love to others as we think more about them and less about ourselves.

We recognize the importance of living undistracted, so we can believe and notice the best in others and encourage them to become who they were designed to be in the Lord.

You and I are now empowered to embrace a new lifestyle as Right-Now Women.

We acknowledge when we live undistracted, we become agents for God to use wherever He places us. This may be at the grocery store, the checkout lane, pumping gas into our cars, picking up our children from school, or even paying for another person's coffee in the drive-through lane. God may use us in ways we cannot expect. This life is an exciting adventure with Him!

We appreciate how living undistracted results in worrying less and praying more. We seek truth and run from lies. We live in God's peace and share it with the world. We notice the little things and don't get caught up in what's unimportant.

We are living our imperfect lives moment-by-moment, guided by God, hope-filled, and focused.

We are Right-Now Women because right now matters.

As we journey forward in our new undistracted realities, we will need each other. We'll need each other to gently remind us when we've slipped back into our old distracted ways. We'll need each other to reach down and extend a hand when we've stumbled and fallen head-first into a new distraction we've not ever experienced. We will also need encouragement, inspiration to keep going, and re-minders we aren't alone in this endeavor. Yes, we need each other on this journey.

We are Right-Now Women because right now matters.

I was recently sharing with our adult kids my concerns regarding an upcoming event I am attending. Every facet began to look unfavorable to me, and my words didn't hide the fact I was nervous about it. I was nearly talking myself out of attending. But mid-sentence, my daughter stopped me. "Mom, you're living distracted."

She was absolutely right. I was allowing the negative possibilities to distract me and to cloud my view of the good God may have in store for me through this event. Sometimes we need another to point out what we can't see. Sometimes it may take someone else to open our eyes to the distraction that's tripping us up. Let's be that someone else for each other.

As we embrace this adventure of living as Right-Now Women, others will take notice. Those around us will recognize something is different about us. They may not fully figure it out on their own, but they'll appreciate our attentiveness and our consideration. They will feel the peace we now possess as we embrace this new way of life, and they will likely desire to experience the same. Not only will our own lives be impacted by living undistracted, but the lives of those around us will also be impacted. Our new reality will influence others' realities. And like my daughter, they might just catch us when we slide back into our old ways.

That's the beauty of living as Right-Now Women. We bring others with us on this journey. We women do everything together, don't we? Goodness, we even go to public restrooms together! The more Right-Now Women we can bring with us on this journey, the more joy we will experience and the deeper our relationships will run. One friend is walking alongside me on this journey. I'm so grateful. We help each other live out our callings as Right-Now Women. We discuss our distractions and how to overcome them, and we spur one another on in love and support. I encourage you to find a friend with whom you can do the same.

So where do we go from here? As we step forward into this adventure of living undistracted, I've shared some reminders below to help us embrace this new reality. It's a creed to live by from this day forward. Each of these declarations reminds us how to live in response to what we've learned. I invite you to refer to this as often as necessary. In the Appendix you can access the printable copy of these Right-Now Women Life Declarations to remind you of this new way of living.

RIGHT-NOW WOMEN LIFE DECLARATIONS

[CHAPTER 1]
We embrace right now, even if we do it imperfectly.

[CHAPTER 2]
We focus on living the abundant life Jesus came to give us.

[CHAPTER 3]
We remove the word busy from our vocabulary and our lives.

[CHAPTER 4]
We address our distractions to effectively overcome them.

[CHAPTER 5]
We understand living distracted is not God's best for us.

[CHAPTER 6]
We partner with God daily.

[CHAPTER 7]
We begin our day with God.

[CHAPTER 8]

We end our day with God.

[CHAPTER 9]

We use simple tools to help us refocus.

[CHAPTER 10]

We keep our focus on God.

[CHAPTER 11]

We use diversions to aid us in daily life.

[CHAPTER 12]

We desire to bless others as we live undistracted.

[CHAPTER 13]

We pray as we work.

[CHAPTER 14]

We believe right now matters.

You and I have much to look forward to in the days to come. We take one step at a time, one moment at a time, allowing God to lead us and mold us into the women He desires us to be: Right-Now Women.

As I'm writing these closing words, I just glanced out our west windows to find the most colorful sunset. *Thank You, God, for being so personal and for reminding me You're with me, even as I write these closing words. If this doesn't confirm Your influence and hand upon this book, then I guess I don't know what does.* You can bet I ran outside and snapped a photo of it. It's definitely one I want to remember.

Friend, right now certainly does matter.

Lord, thank You for opening our eyes and our hearts to a new way of living, one that's centered on You and simplified by living undistracted. Guide us in Your ways in the days to come. Amen.

[PAUSE]

Take a deep breath and pause. Bring your thoughts from wherever they are back to this present moment. Write what impacted you in this chapter and anything you're noticing right now.

_____

_____

_____

_____

_____

_____

_____

[PONDER]

Reflect on what you've learned through these pages and what has impacted you the most. Write down anything that stands out to you.

_____

_____

_____

_____

_____

_____

_____

[PRAY]

Ask God to help you apply what you've learned and show you what steps you are to take next. Ask Him to encourage your heart as you continue this exciting adventure of living as a Right-Now Woman with Him. Write it out here.

_____

_____

_____

_____

_____

_____

[PRAISE]

Thank and praise God for opening your eyes to this new way of living and for what He will do in the days to come as you step out in faith with Him.

_____

_____

_____

_____

_____

_____

Appendix

Access the free printable of *Lord, Help Me Be a Blessing Today* from Chapter 12 at julielefebure.com/resources.

Find the free printable cards containing Scriptures and prayers from Chapter 13 at rightnowmatters.com.

Access the printable of the Right-Now Women Life Declarations from Chapter 14 at rightnowmatters.com.

Do you desire further guidance and support in living as a Right-Now Woman? Check out *Right Now Matters Bible Study: A 28-Day Guided Adventure to Living as a Right-Now Woman* at rightnowmatters.com.

Notes

1. See Genesis 1

2. Henri Nouwen, *You Are the Beloved* (Penguin Random House LLC, 2017), Page 371.

3. Moment (time), Wikipedia Foundation, Inc., 2023, accessed March 16, 2023, https://en.wikipedia.org/wiki/Moment_(time)/.

4. "The Big Impact of Small Interactions," Gallup, Inc., 2023, accessed March 16, 2023, https://news.gallup.com/businessjournal/12916/big-impact-small-interactions.aspx./.

5. Groeschel, Craig, *Twitter.com*. https://twitter.com/craiggroeschel/status/1073785800804970496, accessed 16 February 2023.

6. Adam Gazzaley and Larry D. Rosen, *The Distracted Mind: Ancient Brains in a High-Tech World* (MIT Press, 2016), Pages xiv-xv.

7. "distract." *Dictionary.com*. Random House, Inc. 2022, accessed June 20, 2022. https://www.dictionary.com/browse/distract/.

8. "distract." *Thesaurus.com*. Roget's 21st Century Thesaurus, Third Edition 2013 by the Philip Lief Group, accessed June 20, 2022. https://www.thesaurus.com/browse/distract/.

9. "Let there be 'circadian' light: New study describes science behind best lights to affect sleep, mood and learning," University of Washington Health Sciences/UW Medicine, *ScienceDaily*, accessed June 12, 2022. www.sciencedaily.com/releases/2020/02/200220141731.htm.

10. "busy." *Dictionary.com*. Random House, Inc. 2023, accessed February 9, 2023. https://www.dictionary.com/browse/busy/.

11. "busy." *Thesaurus.com.* Roget's 21st Century Thesaurus, Third Edition 2013 by the Philip Lief Group, accessed February 9, 2023. https://www.thesaurus.com/browse/busy/.

12. "full." *Dictionary.com.* Random House, Inc. 2023, accessed February 9, 2023. https://www.dictionary.com/browse/full/.

13. "full." *Thesaurus.com.* Roget's 21st Century Thesaurus, Third Edition 2013 by the Philip Lief Group, accessed February 9, 2023. https://www.thesaurus.com/browse/full/.

14. Adam Gazzaley and Larry D. Rosen, *The Distracted Mind: Ancient Brains in a High-Tech World* (MIT Press, 2016), Page 6.

15. Harvard University. "Wandering Mind Not a Happy Mind." The Harvard Gazette, accessed July 20, 2022. https://news.harvard.edu/gazette/story/2010/11/wandering-mind-not-a-happy-mind/.

16. Andrew Perrin and Sara Atske, "About Three-in-Ten U.S. Adults Say They Are 'Almost Constantly' online," Pew Research Center, accessed June 4, 2023. https://www.pewresearch.org/short-reads/2021/03/26/about-three-in-ten-u-s-adults-say-they-are-almost-constantly-online/.

17. "multitasking." *Dictionary.com.* Random House, Inc. 2023, accessed June 4, 2023. https://www.dictionary.com/browse/multitask/.

18. "multitasking." *Thesaurus.com.* Roget's 21st Century Thesaurus, Third Edition 2013 by the Philip Lief Group, accessed June 4, 2023. https://www.thesaurus.com/browse/multitask/.

19. Indre Viskontas, Ph.D., The Real Dangers of Multitasking, accessed June 4, 2023. https://www.wondriumdaily.com/real-dangers-multitasking/.

20. Matthew Torin, "Why Multitasking Is a Myth that's Breaking Your Brain and Wasting Your Time," accessed June 4, 2023. https://www.entrepreneur.com/living/why-multitasking-is-a-myth-thats-breaking-your-brain-and/299029.

21. Chris McClure. McClure Coaching, 2023, accessed June 3, 2023. https://mcclurecoaching.com/.

22. Michael J. Breus, Ph.D., "How Your Sleep Can Impact Distraction Levels," Psychology Today, accessed June 4, 2023. https://www.psychologytoday.com/us/blog/sleep-newzzz/201903/how-your-sleep-can-impact-distraction-levels/.

23. "Staying Alert: Incorporating Human Fatigue in Risk Management," Human Factors and Ergonomics Society 2019 Annual Meeting, accessed February 23, 2023. https://journals.sagepub.com/doi/pdf/10.1177/1071181319631012.

24. "Prevalence of Healthy Sleep Duration Among Adults," Center for Disease Control and Prevention, accessed February 23, 2023. https://www.cdc.gov/mmwr/volumes/65/wr/mm6506a1.htm.

25. "Does Warm Milk Help You Sleep?," Sleep Foundation, accessed March, 2023. https://www.sleepfoundation.org/nutrition/does-warm-milk-help-you-sleep.

26. "focus," *Dictionary.com*, Random House, Inc. 2023, accessed June 3, 2023. https://www.dictionary.com/browse/focus/.

27. "focus," *Thesaurus.com*, Roget's 21st Century Thesaurus, Third Edition 2013 by the Philip Lief Group, accessed June 3, 2023. https://www.thesaurus.com/browse/focus/.

28. See Esther 4:14

29. See Ruth 1:16

30. See Luke 1:36-38

31. See Luke 2:36-38

32. See 2 Timothy 1:5

33. "diversion," *The Oxford English Dictionary*, Oxford University Press, 2023, accessed June 6, 2023. https://www.google.com/search?q=diversion.

34. Barbara Rose Furman. *It Is Well With My Soul: My Story* (Xulon Press, 2023), Page 71.

35. Playing Tetris Decreases Drug and Other Cravings in Real World Settings. Science Direct, 2015, accessed May 15, 2023. https://www.sciencedirect.com/science/article/abs/pii/S0306460315002762/.

36. See Nehemiah 2:20

37. Lisa Terkeurst, "But I'm Nothing Like the Proverbs 31 Woman," lysaterkeurst.com, accessed July 19, 2023. https://lysaterkeurst.com/2019/07/15/but-im-nothing-like-the-proverbs-31-woman/.

Acknowledgments

O ne thing I've learned over my years on this earth is I can't do this life on my own. Through the experience of writing *Right Now Matters*, I also learned I can't write a book on my own. Thank you to you who walked with me through this *Right Now Matters* journey. Not just while writing the book, but also for aiding me in becoming a Right-Now Woman. I am grateful for you and for any part you played in helping me learn the ways of living undistracted and for helping me make this book a reality. I praise and thank God for you.

To my tandem and life partner, Bill. I love our life of adventure together. Riding tandem with you is, hands down, the best way to experience God's amazing creation. Team Lefebure is an incredible team! I'm grateful for your continued love, support, encouragement, and presence. Day in and day out, you've helped me to live in the moment and to appreciate what's important. The life experiences we've shared have allowed this book to come to life, and I look forward to many more adventures on and off the tandem together. Thank you for loving me like you do. You truly are my love of a lifetime. I love you.

To Alissa, Morgan, Zach, and Paige. (Morgan and Paige, you know I count you as ours!) You bring joy, fun, and countless smiles into my life daily, and I thank God for how you continue to make our family a priority. I love being your mom and hanging out with you! Thank you, Alissa and Zach, for being easy kids to raise, and for your continued support and love. Morgan and Paige, thank you for fitting in so well with our crazy family and for loving our kids! You all bless me with your presence, support, and encouragement. I love you.

To our grandsons, Nolan and Griffin. Monna loves you so much! You help me see life in fresh ways through your wonder-filled eyes, and you make my life even more exciting and fun. Our days together are priceless to me, and in each one, you help me to embrace right now. I love watching you grow. God has good plans for your lives, and I can't wait to see them unfold.

To Marty, Steve, and Pat. Thank you for your consistent presence and love. Next to Mom and Dad, you were my biggest supporters through the years, and I knew I could always count on you. I know I still can. You are wonderful brothers. Thank you for influencing me to live as a Right-Now Woman. I love you and thank God for you.

To the *Right Now Matters* beta readers team: Tina, Stacie and Deb. Thank you all for the time you offered, for your enduring encouragement, and for helping me polish this book. Tina, thank you for the countless hours you spent helping me edit and re-edit. You went above and beyond, and I'm grateful for you, your talents, your expertise, and your BFFL friendship. Stacie, thank you for allowing God to clearly speak through you regarding the book cover and for the many conversations we shared regarding *Right Now Matters.* Deb, thank you for walking with me through the entire process of this book and for your many Voxer messages filled with friendship, biblical hope, and love.

To Ann Kroeker. Thank you for your excellent training and for the numerous hours you spent helping me brainstorm, plan, and organize the final details and launch of *Right Now Matters.* Your insight is invaluable, and I appreciate you greatly.

To Nina. Thank you for your attention to detail and for helping me with polishing the message of *Right Now Matters*. Your expertise is greatly appreciated.

To the kind readers of my email community, my social media posts, and julielefebure.com, and to the faithful listeners of the Encouragement for Real Life Podcast. Thank you for your encouragement, your presence, and your friendship. It's an honor to journey through life with you through our online spaces. You are the why behind what I do.

To my Savior, Jesus. How do I begin to thank You? I didn't really know what I was doing that evening when I invited You into my heart and my life all those years ago, but I'm immensely grateful I did. Thank You for rescuing me, guiding me, loving me, and never giving up on me. You directed my words and the making of this book. Thank You for prompting me to help other women who struggle with distracted living too. I give You all glory and praise for everything in my life, including *Right Now Matters*. I love You so much. Thank You for loving me.

About the Author

J ulie Lefebure helps women live encouraged and undistracted so they can live joy-filled and abundant lives. She does this through her writing, speaking, and her podcast, the Encouragement for Real Life Podcast. There she offers hope, inspiration, and encouragement based on biblical principles to help women live the lives Jesus came to give them. Julie often speaks at various women's events and groups, and she is the founder, host, and presenter of a local quarterly women's event, "Real Encouragement *LIVE!*" She lives in rural Iowa, is an avid tandem bicyclist with her husband, and enjoys outdoor dining, hanging out with her family, and sunrises and sunsets. Find Julie at julielefebure.com and @julielefebure.

www.ingramcontent.com/pod-product-compliance
Lightning Source LLC
Chambersburg PA
CBHW020241130626
46549CB00005B/2000